OLD SPOUSE'S TALES ABOUT ANIMALS

OLD SPOUSE'S TALES ABOUT ANIMALS

MYTHS ABOUT ANIMALS DISPELLED AND THE TRUE STORY REVEALED

James F. Gaines, DVM

authorHOUSE®

AuthorHouse™ LLC
1663 Liberty Drive
Bloomington, IN 47403
www.authorhouse.com
Phone: 1-800-839-8640

Published by AuthorHouse   12/03/2013

ISBN: 978-1-4918-1020-0 (sc)
ISBN: 978-1-4918-1019-4 (hc)
ISBN: 978-1-4918-1021-7 (e)

Library of Congress Control Number: 2013915733

Contents

ABOUT THE AUTHOR

James F. Gaines, DVM, MS, DIP. ACLAM, LTCOL. USAF RET. has 50 years of experience in Veterinary Medicine. He was the first Air Force Veterinarian into Vietnam and developed the sentry dog medical care program for SE Asia. Dr. Gaines cared for over 500 AF and Army dogs. He designed the kennel system used at over 100 bases in SE Asia. He earned a degree in Lab. Animal Medicine and was assigned to conduct Dental and Medical research with the US Navy. He worked with a variety of species in several fields of medical and dental research. While stationed in Egypt he dealt extensively with the camels used by the Egyptian Army and did research on bats. Upon retiring from the USAF he opened a private practice specializing in birds and exotic animals in addition to dogs and cats. He has bred purebred dogs and for 15 years bred parrots very successfully. He has trained his own working dogs and supervised dog training classes over the years. He has dealt with a great variety of domestic and exotic animals and animal situations and is well qualified to talk about the variety of subjects in this collection of essays.

FOREWORD

This book of essays was written in order to inform people about the many myths about animals. Myths that have been repeated many, many times, handed down by our parents, our teachers, neighbors and friends who did not know anything different.

These oft repeated myths are usually called Old Wives' Tales but many were perpetrated by men and in order to be politically correct I choose to call them OLD SPOUSE'S TALES. Though this title is politically correct some of the essays are not politically correct and for that I do not apologize.

All of the essay titles are the OLD SPOUSE'S TALE or the myth so you have to read the essay to get the truth and the reasoning behind it. There is only one essay that is not an Old Spouse's Tale and that is the one about a merciful end. That is a very serious discussion with no true story, but a heart wrenching situation that every pet owner will face at some point

Some of the myths alluded to in this book will be strenuously objected to by pet owners and those in the various animal professions. And they will object not because of the facts, but because it is a myth that they have seen repeated so many times, read about, or have otherwise come to believe because of repetition over the years.

None of the subjects in the essays come from in-depth, controlled research, but from seeing the "true story" so many times over the years that I decided to share my ideas. A few folks have tried to show me where I was mistaken on some of the ideas but after a discussion and reasoning they usually agreed. Some people will never agree because then they would have to admit they were mistaken and that would damage their self-image.

I am sure that I have a multitude of experiences that most animal professionals have not had. Twenty years in the military traveling and living in other countries and learning two foreign languages, participating in animal research to develop techniques and therapies for treating human conditions, working with the scientists and physicians who were the top experts in their fields, raising and training a number of bird dogs and other breeds, raising and breeding parrots, operating several large laboratory animal colonies with a variety of animals, having the opportunity to hunt and fish around the world, and operating a private Veterinary practice specializing in birds and exotic pets in addition to dogs and cats.

I invite all readers to take a close look at these OLD SPOUSE'S TALES and an even closer look at THE TRUE STORY. Most of you will believe. Some will stay with the myth which is your choice and perfectly OK with me and the rest of the world. But if you advise friends and clients not to follow my True Story advice and the results are less than ideal, then "I told you so" is a very cheap victory.

DISCLAIMER

All descriptions, recommendations, and opinions contained in this work are solely those of the author, are intended solely for the entertainment and edification of the readers and are not meant to be a substitute for competent veterinary care or for professional animal training. In all cases the reader should consult with their own veterinarian or professional animal trainer, and should rely on their professional opinions and advice.

BIOGRAPHY

James F. Gaines, Doctor of Veterinary Medicine; Master of Science, Laboratory Animal Medicine; Diplomate, American College of Laboratory Animal Medicine; Lieutenant Colonel, USAF, Retired.

Dr. Jim Gaines graduated from the University of Georgia, School of Veterinary Medicine in 1962 and received his Master of Science Degree in Laboratory Animal Medicine from Texas A & M University in 1972. He became Board Certified by the American College of Laboratory Animal Medicine in 1974.

He joined the US Air Force directly out of Veterinary School since the military was drafting medics at that point, entering the service with a direct commission as a First Lieutenant. His first several duty stations included Izmir, Turkey, Great Falls, Montana, Cam Ranh Bay, Vietnam, and Luke Air Force Base, Arizona.

Dr. Gaines was the first Air Force Veterinarian to be stationed in Vietnam in 1966. He was caring for approximately 500 German Shepherd sentry dogs belonging to both the Air Force and Army at a number of different bases.

All of the hundred or more sentry dog kennels built in South East Asia were built to the design specifications developed by Dr. Gaines.

He also developed the pharmaceutical inventory and dispensing program for the sentry dogs in Southeast Asia. He was awarded the Bronze Star for Meritorious Service in Vietnam.

While stationed at Luke AFB, Arizona he and another officer operated dog obedience classes for base personnel and their canine pets. This went on for 2 years with over 200 dogs going thru the classes which were full every time they were offered.

From Luke AFB he enrolled in Texas A & M University to do the class work for a Master of Science degree. The second phase of the requirements, which included a research project and class work, was finished at Brooks AFB, San Antonio, Texas in 1972. From there he was assigned to work with the Naval Dental Research Institute at the Great Lakes Naval Training Station, Illinois.

The Naval Dental Research Institute was one of the largest laboratories in the world for dental research. The tax payers have received many dividends from the research done in this Institute in the form of dental devices, dental methods, treatment for various dental maladies, and related medical advancements. Dr. Gaines was an author on 11 peer reviewed scientific articles from the Institute.

Dr. Gaines was instrumental in developing the dental implant that is now in common use in humans around the world. He also was involved in developing the implantable porous tube which is now commonly used in humans to repair severed peripheral nerves.

From Illinois he was transferred to Naval Medical Research Unit 3 in Cairo, Egypt, also called NAMRU3. At that time it was the only US military presence in the Middle East and it had been there since 1946. The focus at NAMRU3 was on infections disease, which insect borne diseases were present and which of the domestic and wild animals harbored and spread the diseases.

One big problem was a parasitic disease of humans called Bilharzia or Schistosomiasis, which was prevalent in the young boys who swam in the many irrigation canals. They were brought to the NAMRU dispensary for treatment. These kids were 7 to 12 years of age and some had their abdomens so distended with fluid that the liver and spleen could be seen thru the stretched abdominal wall. Many of these youngsters also had pellagra because of a mostly corn diet causing a Vitamin B3 or Niacin deficiency. A few days on nutritious food cleared the pellagra. A few weeks on a special anti-parasite medication and they were sent back home where they would again swim in the canals and get re-infected.

Treating these youngsters was done as a service to the community. This and other human and animal diseases which are common in the third world countries, but are rarely, if ever seen in the US, should make us thankful for our advanced medical knowledge.

Dr. Gaines operated a Veterinary practice at each of his duty stations caring for the pets of the military personnel at the station. He has 50 years of experience in dealing with many varieties of animals in innumerable venues and situations.

After retiring from the US Air Force Dr. Gaines went into private practice in Northern Virginia specializing in treating birds and exotic pets plus dogs and cats

After a few years in private practice he recognized a number of disparities in the way cage birds were propagated and raised. He established his own aviary and successfully bred a number of different species of large parrots using methods that preserved the health of the birds, developed a technique to quickly wean fledgling parrots so they could be more easily assimilated into a new home, and developed a much safer, more nutritious, and less expensive diet for caged birds.

His long term experience with a large variety of animals in many situations gives him an insight that very few Veterinarians have the opportunity to develop.

Dr. Gaines is certified as an expert witness for Veterinary matters in two of the largest county court systems in Virginia.

OLD SPOUSE'S TALE:
A DOG'S MOUTH IS CLEAN

THE TRUTH IS:

As a youngster I heard that a dog had a very clean mouth and a good way to clean a wound was to let your dog lick the lesion.

Even today there are people who let their dog lick their mouth and lips. I even saw someone in my clinic let their small dog lick their teeth. YUK!

What if the dog had just gone to the bathroom and licked its rear end or genitals to clean itself. And then there are dogs that will eat the droppings of other dogs. Dog poop is dog poop on the ground or in the dog's mouth.

Do not let a dog or any other pet for that matter, put its mouth, beak, or tongue on your lips or face.

All of my dogs have been taught never to lick any person, even when the person offered their hand. You can teach your dog to do the same.

After handling a pet always wash your hands and teach your children to do the same.

OLD SPOUSE'S TALE: A SCOOTING DOG NEEDS TO HAVE THE ANAL SACS EXPRESSED

THE TRUTH IS:

A dog that is dragging its rear end on the ground or on the carpet is usually taken to the Veterinarian to have the anal sacs expressed. And as folks discover the dog is scooting again very soon. If you watch the dog you will often notice that it also lies around licking its lower forelegs.

The most likely cause of these activities is inhalant allergies. Your pet may be allergic to grasses, dust mites, pollens or any number of other substances. Your Veterinarian will be able to tell if it is allergies or some other insult.

Inhalant allergies are quite common in dogs. If humans ran around with their nose just a few inches above the floor there would be a lot more allergies seen in humans.

There are several ways to treat inhalant allergies. One of them is **not** antihistamines. Antihistamines do not work very well in dogs.

The more common way to treat the allergies is to do allergen testing using either a blood sample or thru a series of injections into the skin and observing the reactions. Check this out with your veterinarian and also do some online homework.

The dog can also be treated with corticosteroids (cortisone) but this group of drugs has some undesirable side effects. The side effects include increased thirst and the resultant frequent urination. The appetite also increases and dogs frequently gain weight on these drugs.

The problem of inhalant allergies in dogs is quite complicated and the only small parts of the puzzle have been worked out so it may take some trial and success treatments to determine what is best for your dog.

OLD SPOUSE'S TALE: ABUSED DOGS HAVE BEEN PHYSICALLY ASSAULTED

THE TRUTH IS:

We often read about abused dogs. These are dogs that are shy and they cower or become defensive when approached or when someone tries to pet them.

These dogs are not physically abused in the sense that they were beaten or kicked around. They were, in breeder jargon, "kennel raised". Most breeders want to sell puppies at 6 to 8 weeks of age. Any remaining pups will be kept together and fed and treated as a group until sold and may or may not receive much human attention. This is kennel raised.

Puppies that are kept in a group after about 9 to 10 weeks of age are likely to become shy and withdrawn. The reason: Puppies imprint on what will be their lifelong identification between 9 and 14 weeks of age. If they spend all their time with litter mates they will imprint on other dogs and humans become the outsider, something that is strange and not to be fully trusted. When they become totally imprinted as a dog they are then essentially wild animals. This total imprint on dogs is not common since there is usually some human interaction. Not all kennel raised dogs will become shy but they will probably be different than a pup that has had human attention on a regular basis.

The most severe form of this total imprinting on other dogs is the "fear biter". This is a dog that will just stand in place and if someone tries to pet it the dog will bite viciously. It is essentially a wild animal. I have had clients present newly acquired pups that were 14 weeks or older with the complaint that it was shy and had snapped at the kids. When placed on the examining table the pups were most uncomfortable because this is the first time they had ever been restrained. When I started the examination and touched the animal they tried to bite with a vengeance because they were afraid. Many people will describe such a dog as "abused" when in reality it has not been socialized with humans.

This situation is extremely rare with pups that were socialized with humans during that critical 9 to 12 weeks of age.

It is not safe to try to train a fearful dog to be a good pet. They are apt to revert to the basic, fearful instincts at any time. A number of folks have called to ask what to do with a dog that attacked one of the children in the family and caused bite wounds, some of which were serious. The option here is to either place the dog with a family with only adults or euthanatize the animal. Such an animal cannot be trusted.

A family dog should never bite a child, or an adult for that matter, regardless of the acts of the person. An innocent toddler should be able to innocently pull the dog's ear or tail or climb on the animal and the dog's option is to move out of the area. If a child is intentionally trying to hurt the animal with a stick or kicking the pet an adult must intervene. My dogs were very good watch dogs and though they never bit anyone, they would have made life miserable for someone who broke into the house. They kept a meter reader out of the back yard. He knocked on the front door and was introduced to the dogs and after that he entered the back yard with no problem.

When one of my best bird dogs, Janie, had pups my daughters were toddlers and they were taught how to handle the puppies and that was OK by the momma dog. When my friends came over to see the pups Janie would allow the adults to handle her babies. If they had their toddler along Janie would leave the pups and essentially herd the toddler away from the pups. No one realized what she was doing. She just stayed between the child and the pups, but never exhibited any anger,

Truly abused dogs are those that have been kept on a chain for extended periods, or beaten for no reason, and other unconscionable acts. These animals are not usually aggressive because they do not realize they have been abused and are not looking for revenge. They are looking for someone to care for them properly and they will return the favor with an abundance of love and devotion.

OLD SPOUSE'S TALE: BIRDS ARE DELICATE

THE TRUTH IS:

Birds as a species are probably among the hardiest animals on the face of the earth. They live in all extremes of climate from hottest to coldest. They are the fastest of all animals. A peregrine falcon (duck hawk) has been clocked in a dive at over 120 MPH.

Birds can live on a variety of diets, many of which are very specialized such as the hummingbird that lives on the nectar of flowers. And the honey guide bird which leads the honey badger to a bees nest and after the badger is finished the bird has its fill of bee larvae and wax. There are many other examples if you care to search.

Some birds will leave the roost in the morning, fly several miles to feed, make another long flight to drink water, then return to the roost to digest food and preen. The whole process is repeated in the afternoon. Some of these birds such as pigeons, ducks, and others fly many miles in a routine day. There are no mammals that can travel this far on a daily basis just to eat and drink.

Airplanes have encountered buzzards and geese at 30,000 feet and penguins have been caught in nets in 300 feet deep in the ocean.

Birds are some of the longest lived species with some parrots living over 100 years. Parrots over 30 years are fairly common.

I had a client with a wild caught Green Wing Macaw that limped. He had noticed the limp when he acquired the bird but figured it would go away. The limp persisted so we X-Rayed the leg. There was a healed fracture. The bird broke its leg while living in the wild and it healed with no outside help.

Some of the very tiny birds have easily fractured bones but only because they are small in comparison with our standards for size. They get into bruising fights with other birds of the same size for mates and come out with only a few feathers missing. The humming bird beak is delicate but it serves the bird well so long as he is not caught by a human. These same birds can fly several hundred miles or more in a day or two during migration. The Arctic tern migrates 12,000 miles twice yearly.

Birds, delicate? An old spouse's tale!

OLD SPOUSE'S TALE: DIFFERENT BREEDS HAVE DIFFERENT TEMPERAMENTS

THE TRUTH IS:

There is little relationship between the breed of dog and its temperament. The temperament of a dog is more closely related to 1. The temperament of the owner; and 2. The age at which it came to be a companion to humans.

I have seen a lot of Pit Bulls in my Veterinary practice and there was only one that was aggressive, and if you met the owner you would know why. The owner was a big guy that was out to show the world he was tough. He had the dog on heavy chain and could barely control it. We got it vaccinated, no one was injured and he left with a more valuable dog since I charge more for unruly patients.

And then there was the nasty Yorkie and a couple of Chihuahuas. They were spoiled brats and a good, loud NO in their face made them sit up and take notice. The owners were impressed also because the dogs then obeyed me. The owners still had brat dogs. Most Yorkies and Chihuahuas that came in were easy to deal with.

The best time to bring a pup into a family is at 7 to 8 weeks of age or younger. Some will say that younger is not good. At about 3 weeks of age pups are weaned and the dam has less and less to do with them because they have very sharp teeth. After 3 weeks of age the only thing the owner can do is feed and clean up because the mother will nurse less and less and will not clean up after them. I have had several pups that came into my home at 4 to 5 weeks of age and they turned out to be fabulous dogs.

Puppies imprint on whatever is going to be their life long identification, human or dog, when they are 9 to 12 weeks old. If they go past this age without going into a human family they are usually maintained as a litter since that is less work for the owner. The pups play together and imprint on the other dogs in litter, not on humans as good pets should do. If the pup comes into a family at 7 weeks of age or so it imprints on humans and usually makes the best pet. Only rarely will such a pup become aggressive and it is usually because the owner has encouraged aggression and has little to do with the breed.

Different breeds are propagated to perform certain tasks but that has little to do with temperament. Border collies have an innate herding instinct, while pointing bird dogs have an inherent instinct to point their quarry. And so on with of the other breeds, but this has nothing to do with temperament. German Shepherds can be trained to attack but are still friendly when not working. If you look up the history of some breeds and the purpose for which they were originally bred you will be surprised.

INTERESTING STORY: During the Vietnam conflict there was a problem with the enemy hiding in the jungle and pulling an ambush. There was also a problem with booby traps and wires to explosive traps across the trails. Pointing bird dogs (English Pointers and English Setters) were trained to detect and go on point when such targets were detected. The problem arose that the dogs could detect the target from a long distance and when they went on point the handler did not know if the target was a few yards or a hundred yards so bird dogs were deleted. The German Shepherd became the dog of choice to work with the troops in that conflict.

Pups that come into the home after about 11 weeks of age may be difficult to assimilate into the family because they are imprinted on dogs and not humans. Dogs that come into the family as juveniles or young adults that have been raised in a litter are more likely to be fearful and bite because they are frightened by unfamiliar people outside of the family. I have dealt with several cases in which a dog attacked and severely injured a child in the family because the child was teasing or playing rough. All of these dogs came into the family as adults of unknown origin.

Any breed of dog that has been socialized with humans as a young puppy will, as an adult, know that if they do not like what the human (child or adult) is doing the option is to leave the area. Aggression toward the family or youngsters is not an option and the dog knows this. The dog will still be a good watch dog and may be aggressive toward strangers.

In a given family the children and the dog, regardless of breed, will have about the same temperament, assuming the dog came into a family as a young pup. If the kids are really nice and polite the dog (and the kids' parents) will be the same. If the children are unruly the dog will have about the same temperament. You can check this out in your own neighborhood or among your relatives. Just think about it for a moment. Actually cats and birds are the same way but more difficult to discern.

OLD SPOUSE'S TALE: CAMELS STORE WATER IN THEIR HUMP

THE TRUTH IS:

I was stationed in Egypt for 3 years, assigned to Navy Medical Research Unit #3. At that time NAMRU3 was the only US military presence in the Middle East, having been there since 1946. The research focus was on infections disease. I had the opportunity to travel the country extensively with a research group led by Ibrahim Helmy. He had been doing this sort of travel for research for over 25 years and could drive across trackless desert and reach our destination with no problem.

Camels can go for more than a month without food or a drink of water. Ibrahim Helmy once took a camel caravan through the Sahara desert (upper Egypt) on a trek that lasted 34 days. Their string of 20 dromedary (single humped) camels did not drink any water for 34 days. They grazed on some of the sparse plants that grow in that arid, hot terrain which has a lot of sand and rock, it only rains every couple of years, and there is no wind.

I have driven thru some of that area on medical research expeditions and there are still tracks from the German tanks of World War II.

Ibrahim Helmy was an accomplished photographer so he had photos of his trip with the camels. He had pictures of the camels just before

13

they reached a water hole and the animals were gaunt, ribs showing, and their abdomens sucked in. They were really pitiful looking animals. None of the camels had died on the trek.

They were allowed to drink as much as they wished. It has been estimated that a thirsty camel can drink as much as 30 gallons of water in just a few minutes. Ibrahim had photos of the animals about 20 minutes after they drank and they looked perfectly normal. They were filled out, the ribs were not showing, there was a bit of a hump and they appeared in good condition.

So, how do they survive for that long with no water? Any other mammal will die of dehydration in a week or less without fluids. Storing water in the hump is an Old Spouse's Tale.

When an animal dies of dehydration it is because the fluid, mainly composed of water, that carries blood cells thru the vessels is depleted. The blood "sludges" or thickens since there is not enough fluid to carry the red blood cells. In turn the blood cannot circulate and the individual perishes.

As the camel uses up its body fluids the red blood cells secrete their fluid, mostly water, into the blood stream, and therefore shrink substantially so that it takes less fluid to transport the cell thru the vessels and the blood does not sludge as in other critters.

The camel stores the water in its red blood cells. The walls of the camel red cells are pliable and permeable to water. There are several billions of red cells so they can hold a lot of water. The red blood cells of other mammals are rigid and not permeable to water.

Now you know the secret of how camels can go for so long without water.

OLD SPOUSE'S TALE: DECLAWING A CAT IS CRUEL

THE TRUTH IS:

There is a lot of controversy here because folks just do not understand the big picture. Some folks say that cats need their claws for protection which is an Old Spouse's Tale.

During many years of Veterinary practice I saw 3 cats that had been killed by dogs. All had broken ribs and puncture wounds in the sides that allowed the lungs and intestines to protrude thru the skin.

All 3 were big males—11 to 13 pounds, 4 to 6 years of age and intact (not castrated) and they had all of their claws. The gist of the story is that a cat is no match for a big dog. A small dog is not a threat to a cat.

When facing a dangerous canine the cat may make a stand, puffed-up fur, hissing and striking with a front paw. The dog barks or feints, the cat tries to run but is caught from behind after a few steps, usually across the back, a couple of shakes by the dog and the cat is history.

I have owned several cats all of which were declawed and neutered as kittens. The surgery was performed by yours truly. Only the front claws were surgically removed, under general anesthesia, and the rear claws left intact. They were tender footed for a day—all ate the next day and used the litter box. The bandages were removed after 24 hours and my pet cats were none the worse for wear. I have declawed several hundred cats, mostly kittens, but some as old as 5 years. The only complication in 2 cases was that the bed from which the claw grows had not been completely removed. A second minor operation and there were no more problems.

A concern is the postsurgical pain after declawing. Yes, there is postsurgical pain and it causes the cat, depending on age, to be tender-footed for 12 to 24 hours after the bandages are removed. I remove the bandages from kittens at 24 hours and for cats over 4 pounds the bandages are removed after 48 hours. The cats will immediately walk tenderly on the front feet and use the litter box. After a couple of days they are jumping up on objects and they are not damaging any furniture.

The best story is about Miller. Miller came to my Veterinary clinic as a 2 week old kitten—wet, muddy, flea infested, cold and hungry. His momma, a barn cat, with claws, and the rest of the litter had been killed by a dog. Somehow this pitiful little guy was spared. We bathed and deflead this little yellow kitten, put him in a cage with a bowl of kitten food and he literally stood on his head in the bowl eating.

I figured I would find someone to give the kitten a good home, until the next day. I was in the cage area talking with a friend and leaned up against the cage with the kitten. There was a small touch on the shoulder, a soft "meow" and I now owned a cat. He was neutered and the front feet declawed at age 6 weeks. I took him home 2 days later and he and my English Setter, Janie II, became the best of friends and that is another story.

Miller grew up and took over the place. He followed me around like a dog. We were best buddies.

I live in a rural area on a wooded lot and we were plagued with squirrels-for awhile. I began finding squirrel tails in the basement stair well. Miller, the declawed cat, was killing adult squirrels on a regular basis. I once saw him pursue a squirrel up into a big tree until the branches got too small for the cat. He also got down by himself. There were never any bird feathers so he did not pursue birds. He often came into my aviary so he knew that I looked after birds so he did not hunt them.

On several occasions he attacked dogs that came into the yard. He would run at them full speed they always turned tail and ran. They could not handle an aggressive 10 pound cat with no front claws.

And he never shredded any drapes, carpets or furniture.

Some folks say that declawing is cruel. Let me tell you what cruel is: A client family purchased new living room furniture, upholstered chair, sofa, etc. They got rid of the old familiar furniture and had the new items installed. Both adults worked outside of the home and the kids were in school. Fluffy was a long haired Persian cat with claws in all 4 feet had always used his scratching post and never bothered the old household items. Fluffy was neutered as a kitten but not declawed because the owners considered that a cruel procedure.

Well, Fluffy was home alone with that new furniture. The parents came home one day and the front of the $3000 sofa was in shreds. Dad grabbed Fluffy by the nape of the neck, opened the front door and the next time the cat touched the ground he had been thrown half way to the street. This was the first time Fluffy had ever been out of doors and now he was relegated to the out of doors for the rest of his life. Now, that is cruel!! They did finally decide to have Fluffy declawed and he was allowed back indoors.

I suggest that in order to preserve your household items and the sanctity of the family that you declaw the cat.

It is best to declaw and neuter cats as juveniles less than 12 weeks. Older cats can be declawed with no danger but the bandages usually stay on a day longer since they have bigger toes and more tissue has been disturbed. After a few days the cat will be walking normally. Complications were very rare and never caused a long term problem.

Declawing a mature cat is preferable to what happened to Fluffy and to a number of other cats who had front claws.

Ask those who object to declawing if they will pay for your damaged furniture, carpets, wall paper, etc., if their scratching posts, plastic claw covers, and other ideas do not stop the destructive behavior.

OLD SPOUSE'S TALE:
DESKUNK A DOG WITH TOMATO JUICE

But there is something that works like a charm. Read on!

THE TRUTH IS:

The common advice to de-skunk a dog is to pour tomato juice over the animal and let it soak for a while.

Yeah! Right! I tried that once when my English Setter, Janie, got sprayed by a skunk while we were visiting relatives in Montana. She stood in a tub while I poured several large cans of tomato juice over a white smelly dog. I ended up with a smelly red dog. As I dipped the juice from the bottom of the tub and poured it over the dog I soaked my arms to the elbow. After a minute or two my arms were burning from the juice. I cannot imagine how uncomfortable the dog was at this point.

After the dog took a swim in the lake behind the house the tomato juice was gone and she was a white, smelly dog again. Fortunately we were there for several more days and the smell wore off, but she stayed outside.

So, what is the best way to de-skunk a dog?

Put about 10 gallons of water in a large tub, bath tub or similar container. Add 3 tablespoons of a no-more-tears type shampoo. Add about 4 tablespoons of liquid chlorine bleach, the same kind used in the laundry. This is the same concentration of bleach that is used to wash clothes and folks put their hands and arms in the machine to adjust the load and push the clothes around on a regular basis. If you go to a public swimming pool the chlorine concentration is about the same as the deskunking solution.

Put a couple of drops of mineral oil, olive oil or eye ointment in each of the dog's eyes. Be sure to use oil or eye ointment to protect the eyes.

Stand the dog in the tub and pour this mixture over the animal. The oil will protect the eyes but use your hand for added protection and the dog will close its eyes. Instead of pouring the solution over the dog's head you may want to sponge the head and face with a towel or sponge loaded with the solution. Wear rubber gloves to protect your skin from the skunk odor. But then the same treatment that works for the dog will work for you.

Note that most dogs get sprayed in the face so that part of the body has to be treated. Pour the mixture over the dog for several minutes and let soak for about 5 minutes. Rinse the whole animal with clear water.

Now you have a normal smelling clean dog again

If you have ferrets there is often an odor that goes with them. Using a very dilute soap and chlorine bleach solution to rinse their cages and bedding will kill the odor.

I have had clients who unintentionally entertained a skunk in some part of their home or garage. And the skunk left its aromatic signature. They sprayed the affected area with a dilute soap and bleach solution and the odor was neutralized.

OLD SPOUSE'S TALE:
DO NOT FEED BONES TO DOGS AND CATS

THE TRUTH IS:

Recommendation: Feed dogs and cats a real cooked bone or two on a regular basis.

In my Veterinary practice I dealt with a number of rescue groups and therefore saw a number of wild animals including foxes, raccoons and other carnivores. Examination of these animals always revealed very clean teeth, even in individuals that were several years old.

The question was why were the teeth of the wild critters so shiny bright while in dogs and cats of similar age there was nearly always an accumulation of calculus (tartar) on the teeth. Calculus is the brown crud that collects on the teeth next to the gums. It is usually the thickest on the back teeth.

The reason the wild critters did not have an accumulation of tartar was that they ate a lot of bones. Of all the wild carnivores brought in there was never a case in which any damage was noted from eating bones.

Most domestic dogs and cats have an accumulation of tartar or calculus on the teeth. This material also collects up under the margins of the gums, causing a chronic infection and a constant shower of bacteria into the blood stream, many of which end up in the kidneys, liver and other organs.

One of the more common causes of death in the older dogs and cats that I saw in my clinic was kidney failure. I believe much of this kidney failure is due to the long standing bacterial insult caused by the chronic gum infection due to calculus. The rate went down after folks started feeding bones.

The simplest solution is to feed bones to your pets. I even feed chicken bones and I am very aware of what our mothers said about feeding chicken bones. The chicken bone myth is an Old Spouse's Tale.

My dogs and cats always had clean teeth because the bones scraped off the plaque before it becomes calculus. Note that bones will remove the brown calculus also. You will most likely need to have the teeth cleaned by your Veterinarian on occasion because bones do not keep the teeth 100% clean. Bones will do a much better job than a tooth brush or rawhide.

All of my dogs and cats have lived to be older than average and none ever died from kidney failure. I have had a number of dogs and cats over the years. All had real bones to eat and there was never any problems caused by eating bones.

There will be people claiming to have seen all sorts of problems with feeding bones to dog. They are over claiming. I had a large number of dogs and cats coming into my clinic and a many of them were eating bones upon my recommendation. I never saw a problem caused by eating bones.

If bones, including chicken (bird) bones were going to cause problems we would have no foxes, raccoons, skunks, wolves, bears, lions, tigers or other wild carnivores. These wild animals eat bone and all when they ingest their prey.

Bones in reasonable amounts will be easily digested by the stomach acid. Note that stomach acid is almost as strong as battery acid.

Dogs and cats will chew bones to granular consistency before swallowing so there is little chance of internal injury from bone splinters. Dogs and cats, under normal circumstances, will not swallow pieces of bone large enough to damage the GI tract.

If you have 2 or more dogs there is frequently a dominant animal that will hoard all of the bones. The subordinate animal, in order to get in on the treat, may swallow a bigger piece of bone without chewing it to pieces. If you have this situation then feed the subordinate animal(s) all by themselves so they can take time to chew the bone and not bolt it down in order to keep it away from the dominant dog.

In over 50 years of practice I have seen only 2 dogs with a problem supposedly caused by eating bones. One was a dog that had a piece of a stick wedged between the upper rows of teeth and the second was in Pug that tried to swallow a chunk of gristle and it stuck in the throat. Both were minor problems and easily treated on the spot. I had several hundreds of dogs coming to my clinic, and saw numerous other dogs around the world, most of whom were eating bones. If bones were going to cause a problem I would have seen it.

I also fed bones to all of my parrots. They love chicken bones and I never let them know that they were munching on relatives. They would eat an entire pork rib bone or chicken bone and go looking for more.

So, feed your dogs and cats cooked bones on a regular basis to keep the teeth clean and promote a long, healthy life.

OLD SPOUSE'S TALE:
DO NOT FEED TABLE FOOD

THE TRUTH IS:

The folks that sell dog food do not want you to feed table food because it cuts into their profit. It is OK to feed table food so long as it does not cause digestive or weight problems with your pet. And the table food must be fed on your terms and not the pet's terms.

The problem usually arises because the pet will find that if it does not eat the commercial pet food the owner will give it table food. That is what is meant by the pet's terms. It is best to mix the food with dog food to insure a balanced diet.

My bird dogs got all of the table scraps plus whatever we brought home in the doggy bag from a restaurant. On the days when there were no table scraps the dogs could eat the regular high quality dog food that was in their bowl or go without. They soon learned that the table food was a treat and it was dog food for dinner if there were no scraps. On occasion they would go for a day or two without eating. Before you form an opinion read the paragraph below about wild carnivores.

All of my dogs have been acquired as 6 to 7 week old puppies. They always had a bowl of commercial dog food available and there was no gorging. They tended to snack during the day and none of my dogs or cats were overweight. Dogs will limit their intake if they know they do not have to compete for food. Many of the dogs that will eat a whole bowl of food and gorge learned that habit while being raised as one of a litter of pups. The owner put down one big bowl of food and each pup had to eat as much as it could as fast as it could. Otherwise it went hungry.

The bottom line is to be sure that your pet eats as much top quality dog food as it does table food. It requires some tough-love. If you feed your dog only fried chicken or some other particular item to the exclusion of dog food then nutritional problems may occur.

Think about wild canines such as wolves, coyotes, foxes, raccoons and others. At times they are forced to go for several days with no food if there is snow, heavy rain, game is scarce and so on. They do not make a kill or kills every day. When food is plentiful they eat well. When food is scarce they go for a time without and do quite well.

When wild canines make a kill such as a deer, rabbit, or other sizeable critter the first part to be eaten is the abdominal contents, i.e., the intestines with the plant materials (most prey animals are herbivores), and the other abdominal organs. They eat the muscle last. If carnivores eat only muscle meat, which has no calcium, they will develop a calcium deficiency which will be fatal. For carnivores that run in groups such as lions, wolves, coyotes, and others, the youngsters frequently die from a calcium deficiency because they have the muscle meat as an exclusive diet, unless they are fortunate enough to get a piece of bone on occasion. The adults eat all of the abdominal organs, intestines and bones where the all important calcium and some other vitamins and minerals are found. They do not share with the young.

Keep in mind that there are many dog owners who feed only table food because it is more economical than commercial dog food. Such pets showed up in my practice and they lived perfectly normal long lives. I never saw any ill effects from a diet of table foods. Keep in mind that the table scraps include meat, bones, bread, vegetables, pasta and so on.

You can also pour used cooking oil, including bacon grease, over the dog food to entice consumption. Dogs and cats do not have a problem with animal fats, such as fatty deposits in the arteries, as do humans. Our pets are designed to handle animal fats with no ill effects.

OLD SPOUSE'S TALE: DO NOT PURCHASE PUPPIES FROM PET STORES

THE TRUTH IS:

The adage that says do not buy puppies from pet stores is totally wrong. Pet store puppies are usually fully guaranteed and can be returned for money back within a certain time. Private breeders will not usually guarantee their pups. While in the pet store they have a lot of human interaction so they are imprinted on humans. Most pet store pups are small to medium breeds and come with breed registration papers. Do not be afraid to ask for references of folks who have purchased pups from your chosen store.

Some pet store puppies may come from "puppy mills", whatever a puppy mill is. One of the major talk show divas made the statement that all pet store puppies are from puppy mills which is blatantly untrue. I doubt that she has ever set foot in privately owned pet store so I do not know what makes her an authority on the subject.

The animal welfare groups denigrate pet stores because it makes good advertising for the ignorant souls that donate to those organizations. Much of the donated money goes to support the opulent lifestyles of the people who direct the non-profit welfare organizations. Little if any of the donated money is actually spent on animal care.

Most of the puppies in pet stores are the smaller breeds. German shepherds, Labs, Collies and the larger breeds are rarely seen for sale in pet stores. There is not an overabundance of small dogs available from any source. If you go to a pound to adopt a dog there will be few, if any, of the small breeds. Most of the dogs up for adoption are larger mixed breed dogs. The momma was a Lab and daddy came from a good neighborhood. The larger intact males usually predominate when it comes to random breeding. See the Old Spouse's Tale "OUTLAWING PUPPY MILLS".

It is unlikely you will get a show grade pup from a pet store, but it will be a registered pure bred that will make a fine family pet.

Regardless of where you purchase a pup be sure to follow the advice put forth in the Old Spouse's Tale "IT'S EASY TO OBTAIN A NEW DOG"

While most private breeders are reputable and conscientious, I have seen some pups from breeders that should never have been offered for sale. Breeders are also where many of the "fear biters" come from since they have been raised with a litter and are imprinted on other dogs instead of humans.

Wild animals do not domesticate very well.

I know this because I raised a coyote that came to me at about 7 days old. I also raised a Turkish grey wolf that was about 2 months old at acquisition and a wild boar piglet that was acquired when about 4 weeks old. All of these animals were tame with me but were afraid and aggressive toward strangers. Fear biter pups that have been kennel raised may do OK with familiar adults but not with strangers or children. Not all kennel raised pups are afraid or aggressive, but they have a different temperament than a pup imprinted on humans.

If you purchase a cross bred pup such as a pomapoo, cockapoo, or other mix then you are getting an unknown because not all pups in such a litter will look the same. They will be good pets but of mixed breeding.

Another reason to frequent pet stores is that the folks that work there become experts in different phases of animal care, be it dogs, cats, lizards, hamsters, birds, fish or other critters. They will be more than willing to share their knowledge.

The owners of the private, independent stores are all animal lovers and animal professionals or they would not be in the business. Check out all of the pet stores in your area and get acquainted with the owners and managers. They can be a wealth of information especially on the unusual pets like fish, reptiles, rodents, and so on

OLD SPOUSE'S'S TALE: DOGS HAVE POOR EYESIGHT

THE TRUTH IS:

The truth is that dogs have very good eyesight and can see colors to some degree. Their problem is that they walk around with their eyes much closer to the ground compared to humans so they cannot see over any object that is above their eye level. A normal sized dog cannot see over a solid fence that is 2 feet high regardless of how good the eyesight is.

My English Setter bird dog, Janie, could spot a bird in the air as far away as I could. While waiting in a blind for doves or ducks I would often day dream but Janie never did. I would notice her perk up and take a look in same directions as she was and sure enough there was a bird coming in.

Dogs, cats, deer and other animals have very good night vision because of a structure in the back of the eye called the tapetum lucidum. This is the organ that reflects light and causes animal eyes to shine when they look into a light, such as car headlights. This structure reflects light, what little there is at night, back thru the retina to increase visual acuity at night. This is why animals can see so much better than humans at night. Being able to see at night also gives the predators the advantage of being able to hunt at night.

But take a look at the animals being hunted such as the rabbit. It has much larger eyes in relation to the size of the head and can see better at night than most predators. The one predator that sees best at night is the owl. Its eyes are large and both are on the front of the face to provide excellent night vision.

Animals have a tough time picking out an inanimate object in a group of objects. An animal in the woods will walk right up to a person sitting absolutely still. But make the slightest move and the animal will be gone. Animals have extremely acute eyesight for movement which is a valuable asset for both the predators and for the animals being preyed upon.

For many animals their best protection against being eaten is camouflage. It is almost impossible to see a cottontail rabbit or a quail sitting in the grass. Most female ducks are brown to match the grasses where they have their nest. The next time you look at a reference book on birds just take a look at the coloration and you can recognize the ones who depend on plumage to blend into nature.

OLD SPOUSE'S TALE: EXTRA FAT ON THE FOOD IS NOT GOOD FOR DOGS

THE TRUTH IS:

Fat in the diet does not cause the same problems in dogs as in humans. Our canine friends do not develop arteriosclerosis (hardening of the arteries), or elevated cholesterol and triglycerides as humans do with too much fat in the diet.

When canine patients come into my clinic with dry skin or poor coat condition and there is no evidence of fleas, skin infection or other irritation the owners were instructed to add fat to the diet. If there was a problem other than dry skin then that problem was addressed and I recommended adding fat to the diet.

The best type of fat to add is animal fat such as bacon grease, butter, cooked fat trimmings from beef and pork and the drippings from roasted meats.

I am not a big fan of adding vegetable oils to dog diets. Vegetable oils are a different type of fat and probably do not convey the same benefits as animal fat. Wild carnivores get some amount of fat from the intestines and abdominal organs of their prey, and from the bone marrow. Fresh bone marrow has a lot of fat and those bones are eaten by the predators.

If your dog is overweight do not reduce the fat in the diet. Reduce the overall amount of food fed on a daily basis. Just because your dog has big brown eyes and is an expert manipulator does not mean that you have to feed it every time it asks. Dogs are as good as children about putting adults on a guilt trip. Do not fall for it!

All of my English Setter bird dogs received generous amounts of fat in the diet. They all had bright, shiny coats and none ever had any skin problems or ear infections. When out hunting they would get hot while running and took advantage of the slightest amount of water to jump in and cool off. All of the mud they got on their coats fell right off when they dried. These bird dogs were mostly white haired and the coats were so smooth and in such good condition that they rarely needed bathing. I attribute their fine coats to plenty of fat in the diet, quality dog food and table food.

OLD SPOUSE'S TALE: FEED WORMS TO WILD BABY BIRDS

THE TRUTH IS:

The pictures you see of an adult bird feeding a worm to the babies are the stuff of an artists' imagination. Most baby birds grow up being fed insects and berries. The robins you see hopping around the yard, stopping to look and listen and then peck at the ground are catching insects. If they happen upon an earth worm they will grab it but that does not happen very often.

If you find a bird that has fallen from the nest and cannot fly the best bet is to put it back in the nest if possible. Do not worry, the parents will care for it after it has been handled.

If you plan to raise the bird yourself there are several things you can do in increase the chances of success. Most rescue organizations are inundated with baby birds in the spring and will probably refer you elsewhere.

If you find a young bird that can manage to fly a bit then that bird was probably the last one hatched and is the youngest of the clutch and needs a few more days to mature. Catch it if you can and keep it for a week or so giving it food and water and then release it when it is bigger and stronger. If left outdoors on its own it will probably die since it cannot escape a predator and cannot cover enough territory to find food and water.

If you find a young or injured hawk, owl, eagle or other bird of prey call the local rescue league to pick up the bird. These species are federally protected and the caretaker must be licensed.

CARING FOR A BABY BIRD: First, keep the foundling warm. Put a layer of tissues or similar paper (not cloth) in the bottom of a shoe box. The tissues can be easily replaced when soiled. Use a pencil or similar item to punch 4 holes in the each side of the box close (about ½ to ¾ inch) to the bottom. This will provide ventilation without allowing the hot air to escape.

Trim ½ inch off of one end of the cover so there is a very small vent at the top. To keep the box at 95 to 98 degrees place it on a folded bath towel on a heating pad on LOW. The towel should be between the box and the heating pad.

Feed the baby canned dog or cat food. Using a small tweezer, grasp a pea sized piece of food, dip it quickly in a cup of water and feed it to the bird. Touch the baby at the corner of the mouth where the upper and lower beak meet and it will usually gape to receive food. Put the food all the way back in the throat so it can be easily swallowed. Don't worry, it will not choke. These babies do not know how to manipulate food into the back of their mouth. It is best to feed the baby every hour or so during the daylight hours.

As the baby grows it will learn to take the food and swallow it. As soon as the baby is walking around place a small shallow dish of water in the box so it will learn to drink. Also keep a small dish with a few pellets of canned dog food in the box and let the baby get hungry enough to look for food. It will not take long to find the food.

The young bird will soon be learning to fly. Be sure there are no ceiling fans, no open hot lights or a hot stove that it may land upon. You may want to keep the bird as a pet if that is legal in your jurisdiction. If you release it out of doors it will stay around for a few days and then join its own kind.

The most fascinating pet birds are crows. If you get a very young one it will become quite tame and be a great pet and they can be trained to come when called and some will talk. Splitting the tongue to induce a crow to talk is an Old Spouse's Tale.

OLD SPOUSE'S TALE: FEED YOUR PET BIRD OR RODENT FRESH VEGETABLES

THE TRUTH IS:

In the wild, birds very seldom eat fresh vegetables. The chance of a flock of parrots (hook bills) descending on a patch of broccoli, lettuce, tomatoes, or other garden offerings for a meal is very unlikely. They may eat from fresh corn still on the stalk, or chew apples on the tree, or grapes on a vine, or millet or sorghum still in a head, but green vegetables is not something that birds eat. About the only wild bird that habitually eats green plants is the goose, and it grazes on green grass.

Vegetables, for all practical purposes, are a foreign food for parrots and most other birds. The most dangerous part is that the vegetables that we buy in the grocery store are not clean, and that is an understatement. In the past few years there have been several outbreaks of E. coli, Salmonella, and other bacterial and parasitic infections traced back to fresh vegetables sold in grocery stores.

While growing in the field, fresh vegetables are visited by many insects, rodents, toads, birds and larger animals none of which are toilet trained. They leave their deposits on and between the vegetable leaves and the deposits are difficult to wash away.

There are feral cats everywhere and the nice, soft, churned dirt between the rows of vegetables makes an ideal litter box. These cats are all infected with a parasite called Toxoplasmosis which comes from eating infected mice. Toxoplasmosis is a danger to pregnant women because it can infect the fetus and cause a number of problems.

Many larger animals that are passing thru or hunting in the vegetable patch leave their deposits in the soil around the plants to be spread on the plants during weeding or cultivation. The folks harvesting the fruits and vegetables may not wish to walk several hundred yards to the nearest port-a-potty and you figure the rest.

If you insist on feeding fresh vegetables then offer items that can be peeled, shelled or shucked such as fresh peas, beans, tomatoes, corn, etc. or items that grow on vines, bushes or trees and do not touch the ground. Canned vegetables are safe but most have a good bit of salt or sugar. If you offer leafy vegetables that are from ground crops then it will be best to microwave them in order to kill any bacteria. They may be a bit wilted but they will be sanitized and safe. The birds will eat the wilted vegetables.

Many folks feed packaged seed which is fine in small amounts. The problem is that to birds the seed is like candy for kids and the birds will hold out for seed and not eat their healthier bird chow. Suggest that seed be fed in small amounts or, even better, only from the hand such as sun flower seed, so that the bird knows that it is a limited food source.

Seed such as millet, oats, wheat, and others are harvested and usually stored in poorly protected bins or even in tarp covered outdoor heaps which are visited regularly by wild rodents and birds that are not toilet trained and never wash their feet so seed can be heavily contaminated.

A lot of owners feed seed and/or raw vegetables to pet hamsters, rats, rabbits and guinea pigs. I used to see many of these pets as patients with fever and diarrhea after eating fresh vegetables. I know of one instance where a well-meaning lab technician in a research laboratory brought in some fresh vegetables and fed them to a number of rabbits involved in a scientific investigation. Within 48 hours most of the rabbits were dead or dying from an intestinal bacterial infection and the investigation had to be terminated. The cost to the investigator was many thousands of dollars

I did my own investigation on bacterial contamination in fresh vegetables purchased from local grocery stores. Head lettuce, cauliflower, broccoli, carrots and frozen mixed vegetables were cultured. All of the samples were contaminated with potentially disease causing bacteria. The frozen mixed vegetables were also contaminated.

Humans have become relatively immune to most of the common bacteria found on fresh fruits and vegetables. But our pets have not developed an immunity and will easily fall ill to many of the germs on fresh produce.

Wash your fruits and vegetables thoroughly before consuming them uncooked. Cooking will kill the bacteria and render the vegetables safe.

Parrots in the wild eat a variety of foods including other smaller birds, dead animals, insects, fruits, nuts and seeds that grow well above the ground on bushes, trees and vines.

The best diet for pet parrots is dry dog and cat food which will be discussed in another chapter.

OLD SPOUSE'S TALE:
FEEDING BABY PARROTS IS DIFFICULT

THE TRUTH IS:

Feeding a baby parrot for the first time can be scary. The little guy is gaping and there is the fear of putting food down the windpipe. The best bet for simple and safe feeding is to use an adequate hypodermic syringe with a large plastic tip the diameter of a pencil, screwed onto the syringe. Be sure to use a LeurLock syringe. A syringe with a plain tip onto which a tip is merely forced on is very dangerous. I have removed several that came loose and ended up in the crop. The plastic tip is inserted down the throat and the food slurry put directly into the crop. Use a tip that is too large to enter the windpipe.

I have worked with a number of breeders who were hand feeding baby parrots and I never saw one that had food in the wind pipe. I saw a number of baby birds that had a burn hole through the crop and skin to the outside because the baby received food that was so hot it burned the crop and it opened to the outside. Such "crop burns" can be surgically repaired but prevention is the best way to go

Go to AvianMedicalCenter.com and see the "Just Like Mom" hand feeding syringes with custom tips.

Some folks use a table spoon that has been bent to form a trough. This is messy and time consuming. If you purchase a young parrot that has already fledged and can use its wings the bird can be weaned in a day.

Some breeders take the babies from the nest at 4 to 5 weeks and hand feed them for 2 weeks and call them "hand fed babies". Well, yes, they may have been hand fed for a short time but they are imprinted on other birds instead of humans and will not make ideal pets.

In my aviary all of the babies were intended to be pets so they were taken from the nest at 8 days just before the eyes opened. That way they became imprinted on humans and made excellent pets. If the babies are left in the nest for the parents to raise because the breeder is not willing to hand feed then they imprint on other birds and you are getting a wild animal.

The babies that I took from the nest at 8 days were placed in a 100 degree incubator and hand fed a cat food slurry. Cat food was used because it is high calorie and packed with nutrients.

Most commercial foods for hand feeding baby parrots must be heated before being fed. It is heated more to sanitize it than it is to cook it. The cat food slurry has already been cooked so it is sanitary. It can be fed at room temperature.

The slurry was prepared by using dry cat food and water mixed in a blender. The consistency of the slurry was adjusted to the age of the babies. Enough slurry can be prepared at one time to feed the baby birds for several days. Keep it in the refrigerator but let it warm to room temperature before feeding. If you are in hurry and must heat the food be sure you can stir it with your finger to insure it is not too hot. Food that is too hot will burn the crop and cause a hole to the outside to develop thru the burned tissue.

In fifteen years and over 300 babies there was never a case of "sour crop" or a burned crop in my aviary operation.

The babies were fledged and weaned at 5 to 6 weeks and were usually in a new home by 7 to 8 weeks eating on their own.

I have had clients hand feeding parrots, from other breeders, that were 6 months old, saying that the bird would just not eat on its own. It will eat on its own if hungry enough and there is food available.

The fledgling babies should be weaned individually. Place the baby in a cage with a wire bottom and a perch several inches above the bottom of the cage. Do this at night so that it gets used to the cage overnight and also gets hungry. In the morning place a large 10 inch diameter ceramic dog bowl containing 4 or 5 pieces of moistened dry dog food. The bowl must be large enough and heavy enough that the bird can walk around in it without turning it over, have sides low enough that the bird can easily get into the bowl but high enough it will not kick the food out. The food should be moist enough to mash with the fingers but not sloppy wet. In a few hours the baby will become hungry enough to start looking for food and it will find the food in the bowl because it is the only thing in the cage small enough to eat. Be sure there is no paper or bedding that the bird can reach. As the bird cleans up the food, add some more and by day 2 the bird is eating and drinking on its own.

The time of weaning is also the time to train it to drink from a water bottle. Once again go to AvianMedicalCenter.com and see the Dr.G's water bottles. When that baby is put in the cage for weaning it will be testing everything in the cage for food. When it takes the tip of the water bottle sipper tube and finds water it now knows where to go for a drink. If you use a Dr. G's glass water bottle the water will stay clean for several days and the bottle can be washed in the dishwasher if necessary. Be sure to give your bird water from a water bottle and not from a bowl.

Water bowls become poop soup very quickly. Some owners say they wash the bowl every day. How often would you have to wash your toilet before you would drink from it?

OLD SPOUSE'S TALE: REGULAR BATHING PREVENTS FLEAS

THE TRUTH IS:

Most animals, including humans, are susceptible to flea bites which cause a lot of irritation and itching. Fleas suck blood and then depart the host to breed and lay eggs. The most common egg depository for the flea is in the carpets of the home where the pets live. The eggs hatch in the carpet after a short time if the temperature is suitable or they can be dormant for a year of more and then hatch. There are stories of people going into a home that has been vacant for a period of time and when they walk on the carpets they will be attacked by hundreds of fleas, a very scary scenario.

If there is a pet in the home the fleas will rarely attack the humans unless there is an especially heavy infestation. If there is an infant in the family as well as a pet it is best to keep the infant off of the floor. Fleas are the intermediate host for the dog tapeworm. I know of several cases where very young children apparently swallowed a flea that was carrying tapeworm eggs, the eggs were released in the intestine of the child and the child started passing tapeworm segments in the stool. The tapeworm will cause no harm over the short term but the emotional state of the parents will be disturbed to say the least. Take the child to your pediatrician for treatment, usually a few pills and the child will be fine.

There are several ways to treat a flea infestation in the home. One is to call an exterminator. They will treat the carpets with an insecticide to kill the adult fleas and a growth inhibitor to keep the flea eggs from hatching. More than one treatment may be required.

A do-it-yourself option is to vacuum the carpets very thoroughly and then sprinkle BORIC ACID POWDER (not BORAX) on the carpets and then work it in with a stiff broom. Boric acid powder is safe. Boric acid solution is used as an eye wash. The boric acid crystals will kill the adult fleas. Vacuum the carpets after a week or so and the flea population should be at a tolerable level and there will be a residue in the carpets that will keep on killing fleas.

If you keep a dog in an outdoor facility be sure that it has a non-heat conducting surface to sleep on, i.e., a board, layers of newspaper, straw or similar. Do not use blankets or rugs unless you wash them regularly. Never make a dog or any other animal sleep on concrete or in a metal barrel or dog house. A metal container in cold weather is like a refrigerator and there is no way for the animal to keep warm. Sprinkle a pet friendly insecticide such as boric acid powder around the area to inhibit fleas.

While treating the premises be sure to treat the pets. One of the pill type systemic pesticides is best. You can also use one of the spot-on insecticides but be sure to read and follow the directions. Be sure to use one that kills fleas because the insecticide spreads thru the skin oils. Since the skin oils are necessary for the spot on preventative to be effective, do not bathe the pet for several days before and after applying the spot-on product.

Flea baths and dips will kill the fleas on the pet but they do not have much residual effect. Remember, the fleas only get onto the pet for a blood meal and then they go into the carpets, cracks in the floor, the molding and other hiding spots to breed, lay eggs, and start the cycle over again. There are many more fleas in the carpeting than there are on the pet.

OLD SPOUSE'S TALE: GENETICALLY MODIFIED FOODS ARE DANGEROUS

THE TRUTH IS:

If genetically modified food is dangerous, then all foods of plant or animal origin are dangerous. Over the millennia all of the animals and plants that are used as food have changed through natural genetic selection for survival in a competitive world. Food animals and plants over the years have been selected, with no man made genetic manipulation by the farmers and scientists for the most desired traits such as faster growth, resistance to drought, better yield and so on.

Today a frying chicken reaches market weight of about 4 pounds in as little as 4 to 5 weeks. In the past it took 12 to 18 weeks to reach market weight. The poultry scientists selected for faster growing chickens, a genetic trait. There was genetic modification but it was all done naturally and over a period of several years.

Beef cattle grow faster and have a higher percentage of lean meat than their ancestors, all because of genetics and there have been no problems. Take a look at the prize bulls of 50 years ago and compare them to the bulls of today. Modern bulls are bigger and bulkier because of selection based on genetic traits.

The same has been done with many food plants. Corn is selected for larger ears, and resistance to disease, resistance to drought and other desirable traits, all through natural genetic selection. It is the same for crops the world over.

Bacteria become resistant to antibiotics because of natural genetic selection.

Scientists have located the genes that control many of the desirable plant and animal traits that if manipulated, make the plant or animal more nutritious, healthier, faster growing, disease resistant or any of a large number of characteristics. Genetic manipulation can make changes happen over a very short term and if it does not produce good results it becomes obvious very quickly.

To date there have been no ill effects seen with genetically modified food stuffs. There are always naysayers who want to see their name in print so they go to great lengths to denigrate advances in the science of genetics. If the manipulation is natural it is OK because nature does not care about the comments of naysayers. They only complain if the manipulation is directed by humans. Genetic manipulation of plants and animals will make the world a better and healthier place. In most third world countries genetic manipulation will give the people better producing crops and make for them a much better life.

As you can see, all plants and animals undergo genetic change over time. Modern science has just sped up the process and made the changes more exact and predictable.

OLD SPOUSE'S TALE: THE MICROSCOPIC AMOUNTS OF GROWTH ENHANCING ANTIBIOTICS FED TO FOOD ANIMALS CAUSE RESISTANT BACTERIA

THE TRUTH IS:

This premise is unfounded and there has been scant evidence of antibiotic resistance from feeding microscopic amounts of growth enhancing antibiotics to food animals. There is a lot of speculation but little proof. Most of the people writing about antibiotic resistant bacteria in animals are not Veterinarians but researchers who are taking bits and pieces from a variety of literature to support their views.

If antibiotic resistance is going to develop it should develop in the animals to which is being fed and it should be to the antibiotics which are being fed. This does not appear to be what is happening. Growth enhancing antibiotics have been fed to food animals for several decades. The resistance should have started showing up long ago if the growth enhancing drugs were the culprit.

I have been a licensed and practicing Veterinarian since 1962 and have treated a variety of animal species from mice to camels in the U.S. and several foreign countries. I have seen little, if any, evidence of antibiotic resistant bacteria in any of the species that I have encountered.

James F. Gaines, DVM

I was in private practice for 16 years and never saw any signs of antibiotic resistance. Half of the animals that I saw were birds and exotics and the other half dogs and cats. It was a busy practice and I saw enough critters with infectious syndromes that if antibiotic resistance was at all common I would have noticed.

Antibiotic resistant bacteria are uncommon in animals. When antibiotics are used therapeutically in animals they are dosed by weight. An 80 pound dog will receive at least 4 times the dose of a 20 pound dog. Birds and exotics (rabbits, turtles, snakes, parrots, miniature pigs, and so on) are also dosed by weight.

All antibiotics have a Minimum Inhibitory Concentration (MIC) which has been determined in laboratories as the concentration of a given antibiotic to kill or inhibit a given bacteria growing on nutrient medium in a petri dish. This concentration is then usually tested on the appropriate induced infections in laboratory animals and an MIC for humans is determined.

The antibiotic dosage for humans is calculated to treat a 154 pound person. A 154 pound person and a 254 pound person will receive the same amount of antibiotic for similar infections. The 254 pound person is receiving 40 per cent less antibiotic per pound body weight than the 154 pound person, or only 60 per cent of the MIC. A 300 pound person will get the same daily dose but only half of the MIC.

Any person who weighs over 154 pounds is being under medicated with antibiotics. Antibiotic dose is per person regardless of weight.

It will literally take an act of congress to make the pharmaceutical companies start dosing by weight. It will be a major under taking because different sizes of pills would have to be manufactured, what will be the weight divisions, and on and on.

Is it any wonder that antibiotic resistance is rampant in humans?

I once posed the following question to a Physician: If I came into the practice with an attached Lyme tick and the "Bulls eye" lesion indicating Lyme infection would I receive a double dose of the appropriate antibiotic since I weighed 246 pounds? The answer was a resounding "No" because that dosage was not recommended. The problem is that if a Physician gave more than the recommended dosage to a heavier person and there was a complication then the lawyers would have a field day.

I personally know of 2 friends with chronic Lyme disease. Both weighed in excess of 250 pounds and had the typical "bulls eye" tick bite lesion when they visited the doctor. They were treated with the recommended dosage of antibiotic appropriate for a 154 pound person and it was not effective. The Lyme organism was not killed or inhibited by the greatly reduced concentration of antibiotic.

With 70 per cent of the people in America being overweight, 30 per cent obese, and still being dosed with antibiotics as if they were 154 pounds it is easy to see why antibiotic resistance is a problem in humans.

James F. Gaines, DVM

It is time for the Government and the Pharmaceutical companies to step up with higher doses and our esteemed lawmakers in Washington to make laws that protect physicians from predatory lawyers when they administer the appropriate dose of antibiotics.

OLD SPOUSE'S TALE: HUNTING IS CRUEL

THE TRUTH IS:

Many folks are against hunting for a number of reasons, the main one being that hunting is cruel.

When a hunter takes an animal, be it an antelope, deer, duck, quail, crocodile, or other critter, the animal dies instantly or within a few minutes. Agreed, there are wounded animals that escape, some to live on and others to die in a short period of time. Most hunters go to great lengths to find and finish a wounded animal. A few hunters do not follow up but that should not label all hunters as not committed to prevent suffering.

Hunters are the reason that wild life is so successful in America. Hunters pay out millions of dollars per year that go directly to wild life conservation. There are very few other sources of money for wild life conservation other that the money that hunters pay for licenses, stamps, taxes on guns, bows and ammunition.

The anti-hunters contribute not a penny to the preservation of game habitat, game management, waterfowl breeding grounds and the myriad of other tasks that go into maintaining the game populations in this country. Nearly all of this support money comes from the hunting public.

There are more deer in the U.S. today than when the Pilgrims landed in the 1600's. More deer are killed by automobiles in this country than by hunters.

Now that there are packs of wolves roaming the western United States the deer and elk populations have suffered dramatic reductions.

When wolves make a kill that is cruel. They frequently tear out the muscles and tendons in the rear legs of a deer or elk so it can no longer support itself. They then begin tearing chunks out of the animal while it is still alive. These predators also kill a large number of baby deer and elk because there is no way for them to escape. That is cruelty brought on by the Conservation Clubs and Societies that insisted on introducing wolves.

The reduction in big game populations means fewer hunters to purchase out of state licenses, fewer outfitters to pay taxes, fewer gun and ammunition purchases to support game management and on and on.

There are a number of Conservation Clubs, Societies, and Humane Organizations that condemn hunting. Not the first one of them contributes any money to wild life conservation other than to bloviate the anti-hunting message. Much of the hundreds of millions of dollars contributed to these mostly tax exempt organizations goes to advertising to bring in more funds and to provide opulent life styles for the people who lead the organizations.

If you wish to contribute to an organization that supports wild life conservation then buy a hunting license and send your donations to Ducks Unlimited, Trout Unlimited, Pheasants Forever, the Rocky Mountain Elk Foundation or a host of other Hunter/Wildlife Conservation organizations the names of which are available online. This money will go to support wildlife and not opulent lifestyles.

Those who object to hunting for any reason are receiving polio and other vaccinations, they use cosmetics and skin care products, wear clothes which have been dyed, eat meat and meat products and utilize other day to day accoutrements. All of the vaccines have been grown on animal tissue cells or have been tested in animals, dyes are all tested in animals and of course the steak for dinner came from a steer which was killed for its meat. The anti-hunters just hire their killing done.

OLD SPOUSE'S TALE:
I TAKE MY DOG/CAT/BIRD/PET TO
THE VET ONLY WHEN IT IS SICK

THE TRUTH IS:

The cheapest pet insurance you can have is a regular checkup for your pet by a Veterinarian. By taking your pet as soon as it comes to your home, or before it arrives at your home in the case of newly acquired pet, you will establish a relationship with your Vet. Depending on your experience with pets the Doctor will give advice that will prevent disease and keep your pet in good health for the long term.

Unless you have a lot of experience with the type of pet you plan to bring home it will be to your advantage to schedule a visit to the Vet. Clinic to find out the pros and cons of the pet(s) you plan to bring home. That way you can make a wise choice at the pet store, breeder or shelter. Once the pet crosses your threshold it is your pet, a part of your family and you will have to live with any undesired consequences. Veterinarians are founts of knowledge and will gladly share and advise.

Another reason to have a relationship with a Veterinarian is so that if you have question about feeding, fleas, water, and so on you can call and many times get an answer over the phone. If you call up as a stranger you will most likely be asked to bring the pet in so they can take a look, get a history, meet you and the family and make you a valued client.

Cost of care is a concern for many pet owners. Pets are not cheap so you must be prepared to pay for needed care. If you cannot afford to care for a pet do not get one. I do not know of any pets whose maintenance is free. A dog or cat will cost several hundred dollars per year for food, vaccines, and medications to prevent fleas and heartworms and miscellaneous items.

There are not many Veterinary Clinics that care for birds and exotics so it will pay to look around and ask friends who have similar pets where they go. Then make an appointment and go meet the Doctor so that when you do have to take an exotic pet to the Vet. you have a relationship already established.

One of the best ways to determine if your dog is ill is to take its rectal temperature. Purchase a RECTAL thermometer that reads in the Fahrenheit scale at your local drug store. To take the dogs temperature it will have to be standing or lying on its side. If it is a small dog it is best to put it up on a table. Wet the thermometer with tap water. Lift the tail and gently push the thermometer into the anal opening and thru the big muscle that controls the opening. Put the thermometer straight into the rectum about one to two inches. If there is any resistance do not force it because there may be a blockage. If there is resistance other than a bolus of stool material take the dog to your veterinarian.

The normal rectal temperature for dogs is 102. If the temperature is over 102 take it again after 30 minutes to be sure of the reading. If it is a bit under 102 and the dog is up and about there is no cause for concern.

If you call your Veterinarian about a possibly sick dog and you know the rectal temperature it helps the Doctor in making a decision.

GET TO KNOW YOUR VETERINARIAN!

OLD SPOUSE'S TALE: IF A PUP CHEWS A SHOE SPANK HIM WITH IT AS A LESSON

THE TRUTH IS:

Hitting a pup with your $1000.00 chewed up Gucci slipper will only teach the pup to stay away from you if you have a shoe in your hand. The pup does not have the organized thinking to connect chewing the shoe and getting hit with it.

The best way I have found to discipline a pup to stay away from shoes and other non-chewable is to set him up and scare the bejebbers out of him from a distance. Now, this is about tough love and not shaking a finger and saying no, no!

Roll up a section of a newspaper and put a rubber band around it so that you have a light weight object to throw at the pup. I carried the paper in my hip pocket and it took only 1 or 2 "lessons" to get the point across. Drop a shoe on the floor where the pup is sure to find it. As soon as he starts to get interested in the shoe shout "NO" and throw the newspaper on the floor next to the pup. It will cause no injury if you hit the pup, but she will know that the shoe is off limits (see "doggy think" in the essay on training a pup). By doing this in the early stages of training the pup associates "no" with a threatening object. The next time you say "no" the pup will back off in a hurry.

This same newspaper trick will work with house breaking, getting on the furniture, and other undesirable acts. The whole intent of this exercise with the newspaper is to get the dog to learn quickly that "NO" means "NO" and to stop doing what it is they are doing instantly. It will take only a couple of newspaper episodes for the dog to learn the meaning of "no". Once the pup learns that "no" means stop whatever it is doing everything will become routine. They will also associate the "NO" command with any shoe that is left lying around. Many dogs learn to obey the "NO" command better than the kids!

You will be thankful when your dog obeys the "no" command the first time it starts to go into the street with traffic going by. A "no" command should stop him instantly and keep her from going into the street. Most dogs only get hit by a car one time!

My dogs learned that a "psst" means no and they come to me and sit at heel for a pat on the head. The dog obeyed a command and the reward is a pat on the head. Your dog can do the same.

Do not go over to the perplexed pup and pet it. The pup will learn to do something to get reprimanded so it will get petted. After a minute or so call the pup to you and give it pat on the head for having obeyed the "come" command.

This may seem odd but I had a client with a dog that learned to urinate on the floor when the Dad of the family came home from work each day. The dad would scream at the pup who would then run to one of the kids who picked it up and carried it around for a period. Dogs are very good at training owners.

Never give a dog an old shoe to chew on. The same for other objects such as dolls, baseballs, and so on. The dog does not know the difference between an old shoe and a pair of new Air Jordans.

OLD SPOUSE'S TALE:
IT'S DIFFICULT TO TRAIN A NEW PUPPY

THE TRUTH IS:

So you have a new puppy and all it wants to do is play, which is good. One thing not to do is play tug of war with a rope, towel, etc. That teaches the pup that it is OK to resist the Alpha, who is any human, and as it grows older it may not want to give up a possession without resistance and for a pet that is no-no.

Dogs are pack animal just like wolves, coyotes, hyenas and other canines that run in groups. There is a hierarchy in every pack and the subordinate animal follow the lead of the alphas or pack leaders. If they do not follow they will die or be injured or punished by either the prey or a dominant pack member. They learn early in life to follow the leader of the pack.

To your dog you and other humans are the alphas, the leader of the pack and are dominant. If you are not dominant then your dog will have its way and become the alpha. This is what happens when you read about owners or family members being attacked by their own dog(s). When I was in practice there were several dogs that came in which were dominant to their owners.

One family had a spaniel that would sleep on the bed and attack if they tried to shoo it off. It was dominant and nasty toward the owners. When it came into my hospital I took the leash and it went onto the mechanical exam table, which was lowered to floor level, all in one motion. He did not have time to object. The table was raised to normal height and the dog obeyed me with no problem. I showed the dog in a few seconds who was the alpha and there was no argument. The owners were impressed and they were advised that they could very easily do the same thing.

To insure that your dog obeys it must consider you the alpha leader in no uncertain terms. Your dog must think, in doggy think, that if he does not follow your lead he is going to die or be severely injured or punished the same as in a wild setting. This sounds cruel but we are talking about doggy think which is the world in which your dog lives. I do not advocate being mean to the dog, hitting it or any other physical abuse. It is all basic psychology. Dogs are not children to which something can be explained. You have to operate in the dog's world to make it do your bidding.

Consider a parable here in that your child has to do some chores to earn an allowance. Your dog has to earn pats on the head which are going to be the reward, or allowance, for obeying the alpha. Remember that all the people in the house are alphas, even the youngest child and the dog must learn that.

Dogs do not have a problem with being at the bottom of the hierarchy in the family. They just want to know where their place is so there no stress on their part.

The first 2 commands to teach are "come" and "no" which may literally save the dog's life one day. If it is going into the street and a car is coming the dog must obey the "come" command immediately or there may be a tragedy. The "NO" command works the same way if the dog is about sniff a snake or other hazard or do something that has undesirable consequences.

Most children have to earn their allowance by taking out the trash, washing dishes, cleaning their room and so on. For pups their allowance is a pat on the head. Not a rub under the neck or belly, but a pat on the head. Watch the wild life movies and the alphas of the pack reward the subordinates by touching them on top of the head with their chin.

Pups need to be set up so they can easily obey the command to come and they get their allowance, a pat on the head. They do not get a pat on the head just because they jump on the sofa and come into your lap. This is where tough love comes into play.

When the new pup comes on the sofa for an unearned pat put it on the floor and push it away. As it leaves, call it by name and tell it to come or come here. When it obeys that command it gets its allowance, a pat on the head.

Any time the pup is away from you tell it to come and when it obeys the command it gets the pat on the head. This only has to go on for a week or so and the puppy will be so eager to obey commands and receives a pat on the head it becomes easily teachable.

A pat on the head goes a lot farther than a bit of food as a reward.

But you must remember in the beginning to be sure the pup earns its pat by obeying a command. The pup receives no pat it has not earned just like the kids only got their allowance when it was earned.

Never, never, never call your dog to you and then punish it. One punishment when obeying the "come" command will kill a thousand pats on the head. The "no" command is the punishment vehicle.

To teach the "no" command see the part using a rolled up newspaper in the Tale "IF A PUP CHEWS A SHOE".

The humans in the home are the alphas and the pets are the subordinates at all times. If a dog is getting too much attention from a toddler such as pulling the ears, climbing on the dog, taking its food and so on, the dog's option is to get up and move away. It is never allowed to growl or bite regardless of what a person does to it. If a person starts being intentionally cruel and causing pain the dog should be able to escape and hopefully another person will attend to the offending person in no uncertain terms.

OLD SPOUSE'S TALE:
IT'S EASY TO OBTAIN A NEW DOG

THE TRUTH IS:

On occasion a dog will wander up to your home and hang around for a while and then it becomes your dog. But usually it's a bit more involved, especially when the kids are part of the equation. The kid's promise to care for the new dog, cat, bird, hamster, etc. will last only a short time and then mom is the caretaker.

If you do not wish to go thru the job of training a young pup then by all means adopt an adult animal. Very few breeders sell adult dogs unless they are trained hunters, retrievers, sniffer dogs or other special use animal. It is probably best to adopt from an established shelter.

Reserve the option of taking the dog to a Veterinarian for an exam and the option to return the animal within a reasonable time if it turns out to be a carpet chewer, destroys furniture, and tears up the house when left alone, or some other undesirable trait that could not be detected at the shelter.

Many of the dogs at shelters have been given up for a reason! Just be sure that the dog is OK with kids and when you put your hand out the dog puts its head up to be petted. If the dog is shy or withdrawn do not take it home because you feel sorry for it. There may be other problems.

One of the problems with adopting from a shelter is that many of the dogs are big and shaggy. Small dogs are a rarity at shelters and if one is present there will be long line wanting to adopt.

If you are going to buy a puppy there is a process. Pet stores are a good source for pups unless you want a specific breed for hunting, herding, and so on. The pups have most likely been seen by a Veterinarian and by being on display in a pet store there is plenty of human interaction which causes the pups to imprint on humans. Most pet stores will also guarantee the health of the pup and the purebred pups will be registered. If there is a Veterinary clinic associated with the pet store there may even be a price break on vaccinations, spay/ neuter, and other medical treatments.

If you buy from a breeder then you need to be a bit more careful. Most breeders are reputable but I have seen breeders propagate Labrador Retrievers that were known to carry the hip dysplasia gene. They may have papers showing that the parents are hip dysplasia free but be sure to check the ID numbers against the parents of your pup. Most breeders are honest but if you pay several hundred to a thousand or more dollars for a puppy that is misrepresented then you are stuck. Be sure to ask for references for other people who have purchased pups from this breeder.

The best way to get a good pup is to make arrangements to first examine the pups when they are about four weeks old. Pick your pup at 6 weeks and take it home at 8 weeks of age, but never older than nine weeks. If the owner will allow it and there is no state law that interferes take the pup home at 5 weeks of age. Pups are weaned by the momma dog at about 3 week so after that the only thing the owner does is feed the pups and clean up after them. You can do that at your home. After nine weeks of age the pup becomes imprinted on its littermates and may be more difficult to train.

Make a Saturday morning appointment with your Veterinarian for a new puppy checkup. Pick up your pup first thing Saturday morning and pay with a check or credit card. Just one adult in the family should perform the task of picking up the pup and taking it for the checkup. Take the pup to the Veterinarian on the WAY HOME. Then if something is found to be amiss with the health of the pup it can be immediately returned to the breeder for a refund. Many breeders will not allow a pup to be returned and will not give a refund. Since it is Saturday morning you can return the pup and stop payment on the check or credit card.

Neither the pet stores nor breeders will pay any veterinary bills.

The reason for just one adult picking up the pup and taking it to the Veterinarian on the way home is that if the kids are along it is YOUR pup once it is in the car. If you take it home with no exam and it crosses your threshold it is YOUR pup regardless of physical or psychological abnormalities. The kids will see to that.

OLD SPOUSE'S TALE:
IT'S OK IF MY DOG IS A LITTLE BIT CHUBBY

THE TRUTH IS:

Dogs can become overweight as easily as humans. In a normal weight dog the ribs should be easily felt under the skin. If you can feel a layer of fat over the ribs it is time for a diet and some exercise.

Obesity causes a number of health risks, the main risk being arthritis of the hips in dogs over 40 pounds. Gross obesity will cause similar problems in dogs that are normally smaller.

Dog hips are very poorly designed and the larger the dog then the sooner hip problems become evident. This does not include hip dysplasia which is a hereditary condition and depending on the severity of the disease may cause problems at an early age. Nearly all dogs will develop hip problems if they live long enough.

There is a surgical procedure to correct hip dysplasia but the dog will not be able to jump after the procedure. Surgery to correct arthritis of the hips caused by inflammation the joint with extra bony growth around the joint is not usually attempted.

Larger dogs develop arthritis of the hips because of their size and weight even if they are not overweight. The heavier the dog, the sooner hip problems become evident. This is one of the best reasons to keep large dogs on the thin side. If the large dog is maintained at the lowest healthy weight the hips will be preserved longer.

Putting a dog or cat on a diet is almost as difficult as putting yourself on a diet. The only way is to feed less food and then the dog begs because it is hungry and someone in the family will give in. One way to reduce hunger soon after a meal is to feed dry dog food spread out in a large, flat baking pan. If the kibbles are spread out the dog can eat only one at a time and it will prevent the dog from becoming hungry again very soon.

Another method is to give a good sized cooked bone. There are some large cattle leg bones available in pet stores. They will keep the dog busy for hours and they are low calorie. The bone will also clean the teeth. You feed other bones that can be chewed up and swallowed on a regular basis and they are low calorie and will give a sense of fullness.

If an older dog becomes reluctant to get up and walk be sure to have it examined by your Veterinarian in order to find the reason. If the cause is arthritis of the hips the dog must be forced to exercise on a regular basis. Your Veterinarian will prescribe a pain relief medication or you can give buffered aspirin twice a day. Aspirin is a wonder drug for chronic pain in dogs.

If you do not force the dog to exercise it will lie around and the leg muscles will waste away and soon it will not have the strength to rise and go do its business. Then comes decision time on what is next for your pet. Once the leg muscles have wasted away it is almost impossible to build them up again.

It has been found that if the larger breed pups are raised from weaning on adult dog food there is a lower incidence and later onset of hip problems as they get older. This does not include hip dysplasia.

The large breed pup that is fed an adult diet from 6 weeks of age will grow slower that its siblings but will reach the same adult weight a little later. The pay—off is preservation of the hips to an older age.

OLD SPOUSE'S TALE: MOMMA DOGS CAN CARE FOR LARGE LITTERS

THE TRUTH IS:

Dogs giving birth to more than 6 offspring will definitely need help raising the young. A bitch can nurse no more than 6 babies without problems. If a bitch must nurse more than 6 pups the babies will be undernourished and the mothers will be nutritionally exhausted. Depending on the breed of dog the pups will double in weight in the first couple of weeks. That takes a lot of milk. If your pet has more than 6 young then you will need to do supplemental feeding.

Artificial bitch's milk is available at pet stores along with nursing bottles. Just read and follow the directions. If you have a very large litter you may want to have your Veterinarian or a person experienced in raising puppies teach you how to tube feed. This consists of using a small rubber catheter attached to a hypodermic syringe to feed the pups. The tube is inserted down the throat and into the stomach and a small amount of warm milk is injected into the stomach. Be sure not to inject much air. It will take only a few minutes to feed 10 puppies.

Be sure to feed the bitch all she wants to eat while she is nursing because they are expending large amounts of energy producing milk for the puppies. I always fed my bird dogs free choice puppy food while they were nursing along with plenty of table scraps.

Feed all of the pups 3 or 4 times a day and let them nurse the rest of the time. It seems there is always a runt or two and they need more frequent feeding since they cannot compete well with the larger pups. If you feed them every hour during the day they will catch up with the rest of the litter in 2 weeks or so.

It is best to let the bitch whelp (give birth) and raise the pups on a thick layer of newspaper inside of a box with sides or an opening cut low enough so the bitch can get in and out without dragging her nipples on the sides of the box. The sides must be high enough though so the pups cannot crawl out of the box. The newspaper works well to insulate the pups from the cold floor and it is easy to clean. The bitch will clean up after the pups until they are about 3 weeks old and start eating solid food. Blankets are nice and cuddly but the pups will crawl under and get lost and become cold or they could suffocate. Blankets cannot be licked clean by the bitch while newspaper can be and newspaper can be easily changed as needed.

When the pups are about 3 weeks old and have teeth the bitch will start nursing less and less. It is now up to the owner to start feeding the pups.

Mix some puppy food with milk so it is the consistency of thin gravy. Pour the slurry into a large flat—bottomed pan so it is covers the bottom of the pan and just stand the pups in it 2 or 3 at a time. It may take a couple of sessions for them to figure it out but they will. The bitch will clean up the puppies after they have been standing in the food pan. You will have to feed the puppies away from the bitch because she will eat more than her share if she has the chance.

If you are going to sell the puppies be sure to have potential owners make a sizeable non-refundable deposit on the pup they want just to be sure they are serious about taking a puppy. I always sent the pups to their new home when they were 5 weeks old to be sure they imprinted on the new family and I never had any problems. I did not ship puppies by commercial carrier until they were 8 weeks of age in accordance with applicable laws.

OLD SPOUSE'S TALE: USING ANIMALS FOR MEDICAL RESEARCH IS CRUEL

THE TRUTH IS:

Most of the preservatives and additives in store bought foods, the dyes in your clothes, your skin care and cosmetic products, vaccines, medications, shampoos, deodorant, toothpaste and other products used in day to day living have been tested for safety in laboratory animals. Most animal research is done for the benefit of humans in all walks of life and 99% of the animals used in medical research are mice and rats.

The animals that are used in research are adequately protected by the law and the Veterinarians who care for them. I am Board Certified by the American College of Laboratory Animal Medicine so I have the credentials and experience to speak about the animals used in research.

There have been articles about the suffering of animals used in research, some with horrific photos of burns, gunshot wounds, and other graphic pictures. The commentary with the photos stated that this is the sort of thing that is done when animals are used for medical research. The pictured wounds would have to have been incidental to an accident of some sort or else intentionally caused by the author or his/her sponsor in order to vilify animal research. The wounds and injuries that I have seen promoted as research investigations by the humane organizations would have no place in bona fide medical research. Note that when they show these horrific lesions they never reference where it occurred.

There has been research done on gunshot wounds. The subject animals were goats and pigs which were under general anesthesia when the wound was made and they were never allowed to awaken. Much of the research on wounds is done when an animal is involved in an accident or other trauma (auto, shooting, falls, poisoning, and similar). Mice have been used to show that stem cell therapy can help repair a severed spinal cord. Such wounds were surgically induced in anesthetized mice and when treated with stem cells they regained much of their original mobility. This procedure cannot be tried in humans in the US because of the medical tort laws. The procedure is being investigated with degrees of success in other countries.

Case in point: There was a recent news story about a meat packing operation mistreating cattle. The surreptitious photo from the humane association accusing the business of maltreatment showed a fork lift next to a Holstein milk cow that was lying down like a cow does when it rests. I assume that the cow was too ill to stand and it had to be moved. If you have to move a 1000 pound cow a fork lift and gentle touch is about the only way to do it. If the humane organization has a better way to move a 1000 pound downer cow that cannot stand on its own they should publish the method.

All meat packing operations have USDA Veterinarians on premises while they are in operation. Inhumane handling of the animals would be immediately halted by these Doctors.

Any business that handles large numbers of animals is going to have some which succumb to a variety of ills and they normally use the most humane and practical way to move the sick animals.

I have participated in many research projects which were of direct benefit to humans. There were 2 basic animal projects that most folks can relate to in addition to other projects that involved dental cavities, tooth transplants, infectious viral disease, and human parasite infestations (Bilharzia in Baboons). Bilharzia is a serious parasite infection in humans in topical countries throughout the middle east, the orient and some South American countries).

One research project in which I participated was the testing of tooth implants in Rhesus monkeys. And these are the same type of implants used in humans today. The monkeys were anesthetized, an impression was made just like in humans. Implants made from different materials were surgically implanted into the jaw bones of the monkeys where teeth had been extracted and allowed to heal. A temporary crown was cemented in place. A permanent crown was manufactured just as for humans and it was used to replace the temporary crown. The monkeys were fed soft food for 3 days to allow the implant to heal into place and then their usual hard foods were offered. The monkeys ate soon after awakening from the oral surgery indicating that pain was minimal. Today the dental implant is very common and there is animal research to thank.

Another project was the repair of severed peripheral nerves such as the nerve injuries that affect the arms and legs of people involved in auto accidents or the severe lacerations that occur when a person smashes their arm thru a plate glass window.

The device being tested was a small porous tube into which each end of a severed nerve in one leg of an anesthetized rat was inserted and the severed ends were cemented with cyanoacrylate (the chemical name for Super Glue which is widely used in human medicine today), the wound was closed and the time for regeneration of function was measured. This tube technique was compared to the conventional method of nerve repair in which the injured part was positioned under a microscope, the severed ends were dissected and then each nerve fiber was individually sutured. The ends being sutured were smaller than a human hair and there were about two dozen ends and each required two sutures. The procedure required 2 hours or more of the neurosurgeon's time and it was nerve wracking work. The porous tube method promoted much faster healing and is widely used today to treat humans. It is faster, more efficient and safer than the old method of suturing the nerve fibers.

Both of these investigations were reported in peer reviewed medical journals and the devices and the techniques are in common use in humans today.

All United States research institutions have Animal Use Committees in place and there is always a humane organization representative on the board. These committees review the methods and the reason for the research. One of the main functions of these committees is to minimize pain and suffering in the subject animals.

The virus used to produce polio vaccine is grown on monkey kidney cells. Polio was a devastating disease until Jonas Salk developed a vaccine by discovering that the polio virus could be grown on Rhesus monkey kidney cells. Other cell culture techniques did not work. If Salk had not developed the vaccine there may be hundreds of people walking around today with portable artificial lungs because other researchers were working on a portable breathing machine.

All human vaccines are tested in animals for a long time before they are tried in humans. It's common sense. Snake and scorpion antivenins are produced in horses. And the list goes on.

The animals used today in medical research live a good life compared to their pet and wild counterparts. When an animal is entered into a research project it very quickly becomes a valuable individual be it a mouse, rat, frog, goldfish, dog, monkey or pig. All of these animals are raised as research animals under very well defined conditions and are quite expensive when purchased by the investigator. They are fed special, well defined foods; many receive ultrapure water, they breathe HEPA filtered air and they are cared for daily by a highly trained technician.

For much of our great quality of life today we can thank the animals used in research.

OLD SPOUSE'S TALE: MILK IS GOOD FOR DOGS

THE TRUTH IS:

Like many humans, dogs are lactose (milk sugar) intolerant after a certain age, about 12 weeks of age. Dogs also do not tolerate regular sugar. Lactose and other sugars that are not digested tend to collect and hold water as they go thru the intestine. The large intestine, where most water is reabsorbed, cannot absorb the water that is held by the sugars. Diarrhea is the result.

If your dog should develop diarrhea **DO NOT** withhold water. It is OK to withhold food for a day or so. Under normal conditions approximately 90% of the water that reaches the large intestine is reabsorbed to be used by the body. So if an animal has diarrhea and water is withheld the animal will dehydrate very quickly because the fluid is not being reabsorbed normally. Remember that fluids are also used up in producing urine, perspiration, saliva and other functions.

Chocolate is also toxic for most pets because it contains caffeine and a chemical called theobromine. A piece or two of chocolate will not likely cause a problem. The problem arises when your dog finds a bag of chocolates and eats the whole thing including the wrappers. If this should happen call your veterinarian immediately. The damage done by theobromine can be irreversible and fatal.

As a side note, I once had an African Grey Parrot, Misty, in my clinic reception area that was very talented and a good talker. To teach her a new trick or word I would use an M&M as a reward. She would do anything for an M&M. I never gave her more than 2 per lesson and there were never any problems. The main part of her diet was dog food. She lived to be 30 years old.

OLD SPOUSE'S TALE: PIT BULLS ARE DANGEROUS

THE TRUTH IS:

Pit Bull Terriers have gained a reputation as being dangerous and it is a gross injustice to the breed and to the conscientious owners of the breed.

As a practicing Veterinarian I have handled a number of Pit Bulls and have had only one which was aggressive. The owner had the dog on a logging chain and he had no control over the behavior of the unneutered male animal. The owner was difficult to deal with also, so the dog mimicked the attitude of the owner. The dog was treated without incident and the owner paid an extra fee for the treatment of the uncontrollable animal.

When I was in practice I had a reputation for taking the dogs and cats that other Veterinarians would not treat because they were aggressive. Most of the aggressive dogs were intact (not neutered or spayed). They were a variety breeds, large and small. The only aggressive Pit Bull has been described above.

Pit Bull attacks are reported in the news. There is never any mention of the attitude or background of the owner, but you can rest assured that the dog most likely had an attitude similar to the owner and the dog was intact (not neutered).

All of the Pit Bulls used in the illicit and repugnant sport of dog fighting are intact males. Most of the owners that have an aggressive Pit Bull or any other breed for that matter, as pets have them in order to show how tough they are. The problem is that Pit Bulls have received a bum rap and have a reputation as a universally aggressive dog. Aggressive people have Pit Bulls because they have the reputation for being aggressive. If the same person had some other breed it would be aggressive also.

I have been bitten or snapped at by dogs on many occasions and it was usually a small dog that the owner said would never bite. Yeah, right! There were several larger dogs that snapped also including a Bloodhound that was dominant to the owner.

Many dogs are dominant to the owner because the owner refuses to reprimand the pet for fear of alienating the dog. Practicing tough love with a dog is not going to alienate the dog. A dog greatest desire is to please the alphas in its life, the human master(s).

Some localities have outlawed Pit Bulls, which is totally ridiculous. If a dog is only half Pit Bull is it illegal? How about one quarter Pit Bull? I suggest that instead they require that Pit Bulls be neutered/ spayed or else pay a very high license fee.(See "OUTLAWING PUPPY MILLS") It may also be required that the dog and the owner go thru a dog obedience school. It must include the owner because it is their ignorance of dog behavior that causes the problem.

Aggressive dogs, regardless of breed, are most often the result of an ignorant or aggressive owner and to ostracize a breed because the owner is grossly ignorant or aggressive is absurd.

OLD SPOUSE'S TALE: CONTROL FERAL CAT COLONY POPULATIONS BY SPAY AND NEUTER

THE TRUTH IS:

This method does not work because additional intact cats, male and female, will show up and the breeding process goes on. And no one can keep track of which cats are spayed or neutered and which are not unless they use ear tags. This attempt at feral cat control is also expensive, even with cut-rate surgery fees.

Here's a better idea. Vasectomize the males. I say males (plural) because in a large colony there may be one or more "sub-colonies" with an embedded male. Most feral colonies will have only one male and he will chase off any other males so long as he is physically able. If the original tom is chased away by a more dominant male then it is time for another vasectomy.

Vasectomy is quite simple in the anesthetized tomcat. Remove one testicle completely. With the second testicle cut a section out of the vas deferens, leaving the rest of the cord and the testicle intact, replace the testicle into the scrotum, close with suture and the cat is sterile but still sexually viable. Male kittens can be neutered as young as 4 weeks of age.

So long as there is a vasectomized dominant tom in the colony there is no reason to spay the queens. Cats are induced ovulators and will go out of heat very shortly after being bred, even by a vasectomized tom. They will not return to estrus for 30 days or more depending on the time of year and length of day light.

This method works because the vasectomized, sterile male(s) will breed the queens and take them out of heat but they will not become pregnant. If kittens start showing up then either a pregnant queen moved in from another location or a new dominant tomcat has moved in.

NOTE: Be sure to vaccinate as many cats as possible for rabies.

OLD SPOUSE'S TALE: WILD PREDATORS SUCH AS HAWKS, WOLVES, SEA LIONS, KILLER WHALES AND SEA GULLS MUST BE PROTECTED

THE TRUTH IS:

In 1972 the use of DDT, a very safe and potent insecticide was banned for a number of reasons, many dubious, depending on the author of the article. One reason was the depletion of some species of birds, especially raptors (hawks, eagles, kites, owls, buzzards and condors). About this same time Federal laws to protect raptors were established and enforcement was started. And today we have an abundance of most species of hawks and owls.

In the area where I live a few miles outside of Washington DC hawks are quite common sitting in dead trees near the road and waiting for prey. There is a pair of Cooper's Hawks that patrol the area around my home. I have seen them take two song birds out of the air in my front yard. Obviously they have taken many others that I have not seen. The Bald Eagle, our national bird, has become so numerous it has been taken off the endangered species list. I do not advocate killing eagles but a nest should not prevent the use of a piece of privately owned land.

So the hawks are back in numbers, in fact in numbers that threaten or have wiped out a number of desirable species. The area where

I live has woods and fields, plenty of cover and food for upland birds(quail, meadow larks, pheasant, and grouse). There is as much cover now as there was 25 years ago when I moved to the area.

There used to be two coveys of quail in the area. When driving around I used to see meadow larks, killdeer, and magpies. Now they are gone. And this is common all over the south east. These species are uncommon to rare in the wild today.

The conservationists and humane organizations say that domestic song bird populations are being depopulated by cats, both feral and with a home. I have my doubts because the raptors have seen the biggest increase in numbers in the past couple of decades.

I blame the overabundance of hawks. Even the big, slow red tail or broad wing hawk can pick off a momma quail or one of the babies as they walk under the tree where they are perched waiting for a meal. The same for the other birds that nest in open fields. The babies and the attending parents get killed by the numerous hawks. Even in areas which have large expanses of fields and hedge rows, there are no open field or upland birds so it is not loss of habitat.

There are areas further to the west of Washington DC where there are very large plantations and horse farms, owned by elite citizens, where wild bobwhite quail are common. There are very few hawks in the area because they cannot withstand the noise of shotguns. Song bids are abundant and there are a large numbers of barn cats.

Hawks, wolves, sea lions, sea gulls and similar predators are pretty to watch but they provide no positive effect for the human population except for the people who sell their photos and the humane and conservation organizations that reap millions of dollars in donations by advertising them.

Every so often there are online videos of a beach with all the little turtle hatchlings headed for the surf, and the sea gulls picking off great numbers of the newly hatched critters before they even get a start in life.

The seagulls are federally protected and present in great numbers on the seashore. Most turtle species are considered severely threatened, but we let the overabundant gulls contribute to the demise of a valuable population of animals.

The main turtle nesting areas are known and the hatching time can be predicted. It would be a simple matter to kill off a few hundred gulls to protect the turtles or take other measures to protect the hatchlings until they get to the water. Why is this not done? The long line fishermen kill a few hundred adult turtles each year and all that happens is complaints. The gulls kill thousands of baby turtles at hatching times on the various beaches of the world. If sea turtle populations are to be maintained and increased, it is time to get serious.

And while we are discussing salt water species, how about the crashed salmon populations in the Northwestern US? The sea lion and seal populations make salmon and other commercially valuable fish a main part of their diet all along the west coast.

There is a large federally protected sea lion population in Puget Sound in Washington State that has decimated the salmon population in the sound. If the sea lion populations were systematically reduced what would be the consequence? The main consequence would be a great rebound in the salmon population. The sea lions would not be missed because they contribute nothing but raw fecal material to the local waters.

The killer whales in Puget Sound target salmon. How many salmon does a 6 ton whale eat in a day?

Other predators also contribute little if anything to the environment or to the economy. Prior to 1972 when there were fewer hawks than today we were not overrun with wild rodents.

The solution would be to put a hunting season on hawks, similar to crows, to stop the unlimited protection on sea lions, and other predators. If predator populations were reduced and controlled there would be a much larger attraction for hunters and anglers who spend enormous amounts of money to legally pursue the game and fish killed by the predators. There would also be more salmon for the commercial fishermen on the west coast.

Wolves have decimated the deer, elk and moose populations in parts of the western US. The big game populations have fallen so much that many hunting guides have gone out of business, which affects many related businesses in the same areas. And the wolves, along with most of the other predators contribute nothing to our wellbeing.

I do not advocate eliminating the predators, but establish hunting seasons with a harvest large enough to allow the more desirable animals such as salmon, quail, deer, elk, and other valuable species to regenerate viable populations

Commercial logging in the Western U.S. was shut down several years ago by the conservationists ostensibly to preserve the nesting sites of the Spotted Owl. These people also have a thing about cutting the trees on our public land.

Many of the trees that were cut during logging operations were diseased or dying. The logged over areas served as firebreaks that help interrupt the spread of the lightning caused fires seen every summer. These sites are replanted after a year of two so it is a renewable resource.

The fires in the Western US during the summer of 2013 have been especially severe because there were no firebreaks from logging operations. The damage has been in the billions with extensive property loss and some loss of life.

Most of these losses occurred because the conservation societies are using their financial and political power to prevent logging and protect the Spotted Owl.

Is the Spotted Own really worth it?

OLD SPOUSE'S TALE: PUPPIES SPAYED OR NEUTERED TOO YOUNG WILL HAVE PROBLEMS LATER ON

THE TRUTH IS:

There is a long standing belief that if female pups are spayed before they go thru one heat period they are likely to develop urinary incontinence when they grow older. Although older female dogs often become incontinent when they reach old age it has nothing to do with the age at which they were spayed.

In fact, spaying female pups or neutering males as young as 6 to 8 weeks is a common practice. There are reports of occasional problems in some of the larger breeds that were spayed/neutered very young. The percentage of dogs showing the problems were very small (less than 10 per cent). These were anecdotal surveys that may not give a true picture of the situation.

If you wait until after the first heat period to spay a female you will likely have a multitude of problems while she is in heat. There will be males hanging around and your female is as eager to visit as they are. If you take your bitch in estrus for a walk there will be males, quite possibly large and aggressive males, attempting to mate with your female even while she is on leash. If you attempt to intervene without a big stick or other weapon the male may attack you. If your female in heat is in a fenced yard the males will come over or through the fence.

An option is to board the female while in heat for about 2 weeks. This is a fairly expensive undertaking in most regions. Boarding a female in heat will incur extra charges.

The easiest solution is to have the female spayed at a young age and prior to the first heat period.

The main reason to neuter a male at a young age is to keep him innocent and out of trouble. An intact (un-neutered) male dog is sexually mature at about 6 months give or take depending on breed and size. Once they experience the male hormones they tend to adopt adult male attitudes and are more likely to roam and to attack another male dog. Many of the dog attacks that you read about are done by adult, male intact dogs. Neutered males make excellent watch dogs. There have a number of instances where a business will keep an intact male for a watch dog and a burglar will just tie up a female in heat to keep the male occupied while they operate as they please.

If you neuter your male pup while young you greatly increase the probability of having a much better pet.

OLD SPOUSE'S TALE:
PUPPY MILLS CAN BE OUTLAWED

THE TRUTH IS:

Puppy mills are vilified in the news, but no one has defined "puppy mill". The ones in the news are usually described as dogs kept in wire cages, the females are constantly pregnant, the pups are not socialized and a number of other ills.

There are a number of breeders that have several or more brood bitches (female canines that produce puppies). The animals are maintained under excellent conditions and they produce purebred, high quality puppies every year. Are these puppy mills?

The animal rescue organizations and others who accept unwanted dogs, cats and other animal urge everyone to adopt a pet instead of buying a pup from a breeder or pet store.

Note that there are thousands of unwanted pets euthanatized in this country every year. It is a nauseating statistic. This statistic indicates that there is an overpopulation of intact dogs.

All of the "puppy mill" photos published by the humane organizations show only small breed pups. There are very few of the smaller breeds in the shelters. Most of the dogs in the shelters are larger mixed breed dogs.

THERE IS A SOLUTION: Convince the powers that be, ie, the state legislature, the county board of supervisors or other government entity with the authority to levy taxes, to create a license fee on intact dogs in the amount of, let's say, $100.00 a year It could be more or less, but significant enough that the macho guy who wants his male dog "to be a man" will not want to afford it.

A license fee in this amount will not be a major problem for legitimate breeders. They will just raise the price of puppies to cover the cost. Breeders who have a larger number of brood animals (puppy mills?) that pump out inexpensive puppies will not be able to afford the tariff and would be put out of business.

Note that I have bred bird dogs and an increased license fee would just be added to the price of the puppies. It is also a tax deductible business expense.

To make this system work a portion of the monies collected would have to be divided among the people doing the enforcement and not just go into the general fund. Otherwise, enforcement will be as lax as it is now.

The enforcers must be rewarded for their efforts. Nearly all Municipal Animal Control facilities are woefully underfunded. I have been a consulting veterinarian for several County Animal Control facilities so I am familiar with the inner workings. If they had a little more money they could do a lot more good and pay a higher wage to attract and keep the best people. They could also purchase new equipment as needed.

If the Animal Control people knew that their work would likely produce more income for their facility they would work much harder to find all the owners of intact dogs by going door to door and asking for a spay/neuter certificate. Few pet owners will pay a high price just to keep their dog a "complete man" or a "complete woman". And the "puppy mills" and back yard breeders will be out of business.

Veterinarians will promote this system because it will bring in more business in the form of spays and neuters. The door to door canvassing will also provide an increase in the rate of rabies vaccinations since that will be checked at the same time.

There are 3 million dogs in Virginia. About 500 thousand are intact. If just one fifth or 20% of these dogs were licensed at $100.00 each the bounty to Virginia would be $10 million. This is a guesstimate but you pick the numbers and do the arithmetic. The money would put the Animal Control entities state treasuries in good shape. Every governor in the country could fit several more millions of dollars into the budget.

OLD SPOUSE'S TALE: REWARD GOOD BEHAVIOR WITH BITS OF FOOD

THE TRUTH IS:

A fellow came into my clinic one day with a dog that was super trained. He put on a show for the folks waiting in the reception area. When he brought the dog into the exam room he started to put on a show for me. The dog was talented. All went well until he ran out of food bits. He gave the dog a command, which was followed but there was no food reward. The dog obeyed one more command with no food reward and then totally ignored the owner.

If your dog knows that you have no bits of food in your pocket it will ignore commands since there is no reward.

The best reward, which you always have with you, is a pat on the head. On the head, not under the neck or on the back. In the wild if a subordinate animal receives a lick on the head from a higher ranking animal it is a big reward.

See the Old Spouse's Tale "IT IS DIFFICULT TO TRAIN A NEW PUP"

OLD SPOUSE'S TALE: RODENTS AND RABBITS NEED TO GNAW TO PREVENT THE TEETH FROM OVERGROWING

THE TRUTH IS:

There is a common misconception that rodents and rabbits need to chew and gnaw to keep the teeth from overgrowing. Nothing could be further from the truth. The teeth of rodents and rabbits are limited in length because of the way they rub together (occlude) and not because of the food they eat.

When I was involved in dental research there were projects with mice, rats and rabbits that required powdered food. No dental problems were noted due to lack of chewable food.

NOTE: Rabbits are not rodents in the classification scheme because they have a different dental formula than rodents. Rabbits are classified as lagomorphs. Great trivia! For this page rodents will include rabbits since the teeth are all very similar except for the dental formula.

Rodents have open rooted teeth. This means that they grow throughout the life of the animal. If an opposing tooth, i.e. an upper tooth for instance, is broken, then the opposing lower tooth will overgrow since it is no longer being worn down, eventually becoming so long that it will penetrate the cheek or prevent the animal from chewing and it will die from starvation.

James F. Gaines, DVM

In a veterinary practice it is common to see rabbits and guinea pigs that have overgrown incisors (the long front teeth) because they do not rub together properly. The teeth can be clipped on a regular basis but the best treatment is to extract the offending teeth and eliminate the problem. Anesthesia is not needed to just trim the incisors but general anesthesia is necessary to extract the incisors. The teeth will not be missed because they are of no use in acquiring food.

If your pet rabbit, guinea pig, rat or other rodent pet has food fall from its mouth when it tries to eat, or it salivates (slobbers) there is a good possibility that one or more of the back teeth (molars) are broken or deformed. Guinea pigs often develop very sharp outer edges on the molars that cause big, raw sores in the cheeks and cause difficulty in eating. They will usually be losing weight.

The only cure for these deformed teeth is to have the teeth trimmed by a veterinarian who specializes in exotic animal medicine. The pet will usually need to be anesthetized for the procedure.

There is no good way to prevent these conditions from occurring. Feeding a lot of good quality hay may help keep the molars from becoming deformed because the molars are used to grind the hay. Overgrown incisors occur most frequently in inbred rabbits (brother/sister, father/daughter matings) that are being bred as show animals.

OLD SPOUSE'S TALE:
SEED IS A GOOD DIET FOR CAGED BIRDS

THE TRUTH IS:

The best diet for most caged birds is not seed or any of the commercial avian diets. There has been very little research done on diets for caged birds, especially parrots, so that any claims made for commercial bird diets are really unproven.

There has been extensive research done on diets for chickens. That 3 pound broiler in the meat case at the grocery store is less than 7 weeks old. Unfortunately, parrots are not chickens for the purpose of comparing nutritional needs.

The standard fare for most small birds such as budgies, cockatiels, finches, etc is seed. Birds are extremely hardy and will do OK, but not great. On seed they will not thrive. All of the egg bound budgies, cockatiels, parrots and other birds that I saw in my Avian/ Exotic Veterinary practice were on seed diets which are deficient in calcium and a number of other nutrients. Some seed vendors tout their "Fresh Seed"; yeah, right. There has been seed recovered from a ten thousand year old tomb and it sprouted when planted. Fresh in the seed world means it will sprout under proper conditions.

If you think about it seed is available to wild birds only in fall and winter. It is a survival diet. Seed will see them thru the winter. Seeds have a high fat content which provides calories and energy in the cold of winter. In the spring when its time to make nests, breed and produce babies there are berries, insects and young shoots available but no seed.

In 1981 I lost a fantastic Congo African Grey parrot that I had purchased as a bronco (wild caught) while stationed in Egypt with the military. After a number of bites to the fingers and hand we finally got an understanding and made friends. This bird would pick up a word or short phrase after about 15 minutes of repetition.

One night I heard the bird fluttering in his cage, then a thump. I turned on the light to find my buddy lying dead in the bottom of the cage. He died from an acute hypocalcemia (low blood calcium) brought on by a seed diet. In those days I did not know much about avian diets and was forced by that bitter experience to do some research.

After looking around in the pet stores and reading the scientific books I found there was little information on avian diets. Hmm! How about dog food? There were some folks at the time saying that dog food contained too much protein and fat, but it was all speculation. If anyone discourages feeding conventional dog or cat food to caged birds ask how long they fed such a diet to their birds before they made that decision. If they never fed such a diet they are speaking from untested theory. My pet birds also received table food such as cooked meat, French fries, and cooked bones.

Another problem with seed is that it can be contaminated with all sorts of animal and insect excretions. Bulk seed such as millet, corn on the cob and shelled corn, wheat, oats, etc. are usually not protected from birds and rodents when stored. Wild pigeons, mice, rats, sparrows and other wild life land on the grain for a meal and use the same venue for a toilet. These stored grains go directly into the bag that you purchase at retail. Some of it is contaminated and there is no way to tell just what sort of dangers may lurk in the "fresh seed' that you acquire.

Shortly after I opened my Veterinary Practice I acquired a teen aged African Grey. It went immediately on dry dog food and did extremely well. After about a year there was no longer a ridge at the tip of the beak and the beak was shiny with no scratches. If you have a hook bill bird (budgie, cockatiel, parrot, etc.) take a look at the beak. It should be shiny and smooth. Most hook bills being fed commercial diets will have a beak with what appear to be flakes on the surface and a ridge at the tip of the beak because the horny layer does not wear off as nature intended due to missing nutrients.

Upon leaving the U.S. Air Force after 20 years of service I started my own Avian/Exotic and Small Animal practice. As an Avian specialist there was a lot of opportunity to acquire a variety of parrots and my breeding aviary was started. There were 3 pairs of macaws, Umbrella cockatoos, Moluccan cockatoos, eclectus, and African Greys. The bulk of the diet was dog food with a handful of roasted peanuts and black oil sunflower seeds once a week. These birds thrived for the 15 years that I maintained the aviary and those birds produced babies like they were chickens.

The babies were taken from the nest at 8 days of age, just before the eyes opened and hand fed with ground cat food mixed in water. This diet was fed by syringe at room temperature. There is no need to heat this mixture because the cat food has already been cooked and does not need to be sterilized. The babies grew faster, fledged earlier and were weaned in 24 hours onto dry dog food that had been moistened enough to make it soft. I stayed in touch with some of the folks who purchased the babies, which made excellent pets, and they were in perfect health 12 years later. This is not a real scientific exercise but the results I had were better that my clients who had breeding aviaries and fed commercial bird diets. Once they switched to dog food the problems went away.

My daughter did a grade school science fair project comparing dog food and seed diets in weanling budgies (parakeets). At 6 weeks of age she put 3 birds on seed and 3 on ground dog food until Science Fair time 6 weeks later. The budgies on seed had yellowish, flaked beaks and rough skin on the feet which most people consider normal because they have never seen a budgie that has had excellent nutrition. The birds fed the dog food had normal bluish, very smooth beaks and smooth skin on the feet.

Take a close look at your bird's beak. Chances are there is ridge at the tip of the beak. If you look closely at the sides of the beak there are numerous scratches. This is usually attributed to rubbing the beak on the perch or other objects. No, no, no~ it's due to a nutritional deficiency. None of the birds that I had in the aviary or pet birds on a dog food diet had these defects. They all had smooth, shiny beaks with no ridge at the tip.

If you have a dog and feed regular dog food, not a reducing diet or medical diet, put your bird on dog food. If you have a cat and feed regular cat food then feed cat food. Give this diet for a year and the beak defects will disappear along with other features which will improve.

Dog and cat food is less expensive to feed than the commercial bird diets, even seed.

Small birds such as budgies, cockatiels, finches, etc must be changed over gradually by mixing ground dog/cat food with their conventional diet and gradually reducing the conventional food.

Large birds can usually be turned over to the new diet by just offering it in a separate food dish and removing all other food from the cage. You will know when they are eating the dog food because they will be passing stool. The stool is the dark part of the dropping. The white part is the urine.

Only ROASTED peanuts should be fed. Raw peanuts of any sort may contain the mold Aspergillus which is highly toxic for birds and is rapidly fatal due to irreversible liver failure.

This dog food diet will not be recommended by pet stores and other folks who sell bird chow because there is much less profit than for seed or commercial bird chow.

OLD SPOUSE'S TALE: SURGICAL DEBARKING IS CRUEL

THE TRUTH IS:

A constantly barking dog is a good way to create angry neighbors. Many times the dog barks when the owners are not at home so they are not aware of the problem except for the complaints. There are electronic collars that deliver a shock when the dog barks but if the battery wears out the dog will quickly figure out it is OK to bark again. The dog can be locked in the house but the noise frequently can be heard from outside the home.

Surgical debarking (medical term: ventriculochordectomy) is considered cruel by some but it is a knee jerk reaction and not an informed opinion. Debarking is normally a very short procedure and it is always done under general anesthesia.

The debarking procedure consists of making a notch in each of the 2 vocal cords. The dog is not rendered mute. When it barks the sound is a cough-like sound or a muffled bark that has little volume. A person knocking on your front door will be able to hear the dog and will just think it is hoarse. The dog can still whine and make sounds, just not at a volume that carries to the neighbors. The reduced volume lasts about 6 months and then as the notch in the vocal cords grows back the volume will return.

Even if the pet persists in "barking" there will not be any volume and most learn to stay quiet.

I speak from experience. I had an English Setter female which was an outstanding bird dog and retriever, and an excellent watch dog. My neighbors told me she would sit in our large fenced yard during the day while the house was empty and bark incessantly. She was debarked (by yours truly) and after the volume returned in about 6 months she stayed quiet while we were away. Problem solved!

OLD SPOUSE'S TALE: TO HOUSE BREAK A DOG RUB HIS NOSE IN THE MESS AND PUT HIM OUTSIDE

THE TRUTH IS:

If a pup has a mistake in the house, sticking his nose in the urine or feces and putting him outside serves no purpose. The pup does not associate the mess with anything it did.

When a new dog comes into the household it is best if it has its own house to live in such as a dog crate. If it is a puppy it can be locked in the crate at night so it does not get into trouble around the house. It is also a good idea to have the same arrangement for an older dog that you adopt until it find its place in the household.

During the day the crate can be left open so the pet can get away into its own domain.

To house break a pup with the intention of teaching it to use the yard as a toilet, put it in a confined area indoors with paper covering the floor. Keep an eye on the pup and as soon as you see it squatting to eliminate give a firm "NO" and pick it up, take it outside, put it on the ground and wait for it to eliminate. Once it is finished pat it on the head as a reward for getting it right (see the Old Spouse's Tale on dog training). Put the pup back in the confined area and wait for it to squat again. You can also take it outside to play and when it eliminates out of doors reward it with a pat on the head and words of encouragement.

If the pup is paper trained in the house you can put a section of newspaper in the yard and when you take the pup out of doors take it to the paper to do its business. I have seen dogs trained to use a piece of paper no larger than a tissue and they never missed.

Teaching the pup to defecate out of doors is fairly simple. Use the "match trick". A little while after the pup has eaten a meal take a single **PAPER** match out of a matchbook. Insert the head end into the rectum (up the butt). It cannot cause any harm. In a minute or so the pup will start looking for a place to defecate. Pick it up or using a leash take it outside to the toilet area and it will eliminate. Once again give a pat on the head and an encouraging word. In a short time the dog will let you know when it has to go outside.

You can actually teach the dog to defecate on command. This will prevent you from having to stand out in the rain waiting for the dog to do its business. As soon as the match starts working give the command "Dump it" or something similar and before long the dog will literally go on command.

I used this match trick on our cat, Rosie, on the way to be stationed with the military in Cairo, Egypt to do medical research. Rosie was part of the family and older than our 2 children at the time. She was laid back and gentle.

We were waiting at JFK airport in New York. Before putting her in the carrier for the trip overseas I held the cat and my wife inserted the match. I think the audience in the waiting area expected fireworks. I carried her outside made my way thru several lanes of traffic to the center island which was choked with weeds and trash.

She was in a harness with a leash. It took a minute or two but she found a suitable patch of dirt, eliminated and dutifully covered it. We then took a short stroll along the median and then she stopped, stared into the weeds for a few seconds, dove in and came out with a mouse. How she detected the mouse with all the traffic and activity I cannot figure. Once in Cairo she quickly adapted and enjoyed the tour.

OLD SPOUSE'S TALE:
USE A BELL TO KEEP THE DOG OR CAT AWAY FROM THE CHRISTMAS TREE, GARBAGE CAN, OFF THE KITCHEN COUNTER, ETC.

THE TRUTH IS:

Cats like to play with dangling Christmas tree ornaments and dogs will rummage thru an open trash can. Dogs will take items from the counter if they are tall enough to reach it. Cats will jump on the counter and other food preparation surfaces to check them out, and in my experience, they do not wash their feet first, even if they have just been to the litter box.

First, the dog dilemma. The trash can may be put into a pull out cabinet or a can with a cover. Both of these pose a problem if you are like me and prefer to be able to toss items in the trash from a distance to avoid walking over to the receptacle, lifting the lid and depositing the item.

The best way to keep pets from all of the locations listed above, and probably some that are less of a problem such as your bed, the furniture and other areas is to use one or more mouse traps.

This method may seem a bit profound but we are trying to keep the dog from eating a big piece of aluminum foil, tin can lid or other foreign material from the trash which will have to be surgically removed for a hefty price.

We are going to keep the cat off of the counter in order to prevent tracking debris from the litter box onto food service areas or helping itself to a thawing piece of meat and to keep the dog from eating food items from the counter.

I have seen other methods suggested such as bells that warn the owner that the pet is transgressing. This may work a time or two but the pet learns to avoid the bells or is gone by the time the owner arrives to give a reprimand. We are talking here about bringing this undesirable behavior to a screeching halt with a bit of tough love. Do not worry; the pet will not associate you with the traps.

I had a distraught newlywed call my Veterinary Hospital and said her diamond ring was missing from the kitchen counter and she thought the dog, a large black Labrador retriever, might have swallowed it. An X-ray showed that she was correct. It was in the large intestine. In a case like this an enema is contraindicated because the dog will defecate in several different places in the yard and it may be difficult to locate the ring in the grass. We used the match trick (see HOUSE BREAKING A PUP) and it worked like a charm. The dog had a bowel movement and a Veterinary Technician, with rubber gloves, quickly found the ring. Fortunately, the dog did not chew the ring before swallowing. Her next step was to put mouse traps on the counter.

The mouse traps are not used to injure the pet, just to frighten them. Apply a few drops of Vanilla extract, Cinnamon, or other aromatic material to the wood of the trap. Do not use a scent from something the pet may eat such as sardines, peanut butter, etc. This may cause the pet to stop eating food that contains that flavor.

Set the trap in the normal manner and place it very gently UPSIDE DOWN in the trash can or on the counter. When the pet touches the trap it will go off and spring up and give them a good scare.

If the pet avoids the trap and still scouts out the counter then use several traps, set upside down but each draped with a single piece of paper towel. When they step on it or sniff the trap it will pop up and give them a good scare. They rarely come back for a second helping.

The reason for applying the liquid aromatic spice is so that once the pet learns to avoid the distinctive odor. The spice can be applied to other pet "no go" areas and the cat or dog will avoid the odor even if there is no trap. The pet will not associate you with the traps unless you spill the aromatic material on yourself.

We had a big grey cat, MishMish, who kept jumping on the dining room table and leaving grey hairs on the white table cloth. I put several mouse traps odorized with Vanilla extract on the table and covered each with a tissue. The cat set off one of the traps and we never had hair on the table cloth again.

To keep pets from playing with the Christmas ornaments place several aromatically enhanced traps around the perimeter of the tree. Once the pet has set off one or the traps then just the aromatic spice will be enough to make them keep their distance.

OLD SPOUSE'S TALE: REMOVE TICKS BY COATING THEM WITH PETROLEUM JELLY SO THEY SUFFOCATE

THE TRUTH IS:

There are many Old Spouse's Tales about how best to remove embedded ticks from dogs such as cover them with petroleum jelly so they suffocate, touch them with a lighted cigarette or hot match so they will back out, and so on. None of these methods serves any purpose.

The most prevalent reason for trying to kill the tick or urge it to back out is so that the head will not be left in the skin. Never fear! Ticks are very tightly attached to their heads. Of the many hundreds of ticks that I have removed manually (pulled out with tweezers) the head has always been attached.

There are a variety of anti-parasite medications that can be administered monthly or as recommended by the manufacturer. These products will kill ticks and fleas, and prevent internal parasites. The problem is that it takes a day or two for ticks to be killed by these products and in that amount of time they can engorge with blood and transmit disease.

To remove a tick from any host animal use sharp pointed tweezers so you can grasp the head end of the tick without squeezing the engorged body of the tick. If you squeeze the engorged body of the tick some of the contents will be injected into the victim and can cause a local infection. If the tick is carrying a disease such as Rocky Mountain spotted fever, Erlichia, Lyme or other malady it is much more likely to transmit the disease. Ticks must attach to the host and begin sucking blood in order to transmit disease.

If your pet becomes laden with scores of ticks it is best to take him to your Veterinarian to be bathed and dipped to kill the ticks. You can purchase dip solutions or animal safe insecticidal sprays at pet stores. Use as directed and after a few hours the ticks can be removed with a comb. Be sure to check the ears, under the tail, the belly and where the legs meet the body.

TICK TRIVIA: Only the female ticks engorge and are the main disease transmitters. If you remove an engorged tick and find a smaller tick at the same site it is a male that has followed the female pheromones to locate and breed with the female. The male tick can detect the female pheromones from several feet away. The female does not emit the pheromones until she is engorged and ready to breed.

OLD SPOUSE'S TALE:
KEEP REPTILES IN A SCREEN
COVERED CAGE

THE TRUTH IS:

The reptile habitats sold by pet stores are most often aquariums with a fitted screen cover and a light bulb for heat. If light bulbs produced enough heat to affect a space then we would not need furnaces and heat pumps. All of the heat from a light bulb rises so the interior of a space is not affected unless it is above the light bulb.

Infrared heat lamps are a bit better but they only heat a small portion of the habitat.

To keep a reptile habitat at the proper temperature of 95 to 99 degrees Fahrenheit the heat source must be under the cage. There are heating devices available in pet stores that attach under the bottom glass of an aquarium to provide adequate warmth for the critter.

You can also place the aquarium on 2 books or boards, one at each end and place a heating pad under the enclosure. Be sure to have in place a stick-on thermometer on the inside of the habitat regardless of the type of heat source. Measuring the temperature on the outside of the glass serves no purpose.

When a reptile is living in a heated habitat with a screen cover it is living in a desert. The heat rises right thru the screen lid taking all of the moisture with it and the bottom of the cage where the reptile lives is the coldest, driest part of the cage.

The best cover for an aquarium habitat is a piece of glass that completely covers the habitat except for a one half inch space at one end, If you have a reptile pet that can jump or climb on the glass, or a snake that can reach the top of the cage, put the glass on top of the screen. The glass will hold the heat and humidity (moisture in the air) inside the cage. When you make this change be sure to monitor the temperature to insure that it does not become too warm.

Place a shallow bowl of water in the bottom of the cage to provide humidity thru evaporation and drinking water for the pet. A ceramic dog bowl works for most species. Be sure to change the water frequently because as it evaporates the minerals become concentrated and over a period of time the water will become salty and unhealthy to drink.

The glass sides of the aquarium should have a small amount of water droplets clinging which indicates that the humidity is adequate.

Many reptiles are nocturnal so they are not active during the day. To observe their activity at night place a blue or red bulb (party bulb) with a reflector next to the cage at night or in a darkened room. With the reflector in place the habitat will be well lit thru the glass and to the reptile it is still dark since they cannot see in a red or blue light.

OLD SPOUSE'S TALE: OUR COMPANY DOES NOT TEST OUR PRODUCTS IN ANIMALS

THE TRUTH IS:

Many manufacturers of cosmetics, home care products, medications and other items claim that they do not test their products in animals. And they are telling the truth; up to a point!

At the present time there are not any computer programs that can completely mimic animal testing even though some of the animal welfare organizations would have you believe otherwise.

Virtually all of the consumable products on the market have some degree of animal testing. This includes the dyes in cloth, food dyes, chemicals, vaccines, antibiotics, and other medications. There is just no other way to study all of the good and bad effects, side effects and other factors that were not even considered in the beginning.

Imagine if a lady sued a cosmetics company because their new product caused eye problems. At the trial her lawyer asks the cosmetics company witness if the product had been tested on animals and the answer was no. The lady just won her case and a large sum of money.

When a manufacturer states that they do not perform animal testing they are speaking the truth, but they have their fingers crossed behind their back. They do not say that their products are not tested in animals. They hire an **outside laboratory** to do the testing in animals.

Now you know the truth.

OLD SPOUSE'S TALE: WEAN ALL PUPPIES ONTO COMMERCIAL PUPPY FOOD

THE TRUTH IS:

The story here is yes and no. Pups are usually started on a solid food diet at about 3 to 4 weeks of age.

The very small breed pups such as Chihuahuas, miniature poodles, Pomeranians and similar are quite susceptible to "sugar shock" or low blood sugar. This is because they have a high metabolic rate and in the beginning have a difficult time taking in enough food to keep up with the energy demands of their body. Nature provides for this difficulty by limiting litters of the very tiny breeds to 2 or 3. The small momma has to produce a lot of milk in relation to her size to raise the pups and a big litter would either kill the momma or some of the pups would starve.

When tiny breed pups came into my clinic they were put on kitten food until they were about 4 months old. Kitten food is high calorie and will meet the caloric needs of the tiny pups. Note that kittens are very small and need a high calorie food.

The medium size breeds that grow to 20 to 40 pounds can be weaned onto regular puppy food. The large breeds that grow to over 40 pounds should be weaned onto a good quality adult food.

Why wean large pups onto adult food? The reason is that large dogs have a lower incidence of hip arthritis (not hip dysplasia which is hereditary and not affected by diet) when they are raised on adult food.

There has been credible research done on this subject. Litters of German Shepherds were divided into 2 groups and one group fed the high calorie puppy food and the other half fed adult food. The pups on adult food took longer than their siblings on puppy food to reach full adult weight but they grew as large as their siblings in the end and had a much lower incidence of hip arthritis as they aged.

OLD SPOUSE'S TALE: WEAN PUPS AT 6 WEEKS

THE TRUTH IS:

Puppies are usually weaned by the momma dog at 3 to 4 weeks of age. That is the age that the teeth have erupted enough to be sharp and momma objects to the pain from exuberant nursing and biting. And by weaning at this age it takes a big load off of the mama dog because she does not have to nurse them as much. It is absolutely necessary to start feeding regular food at about 3 to 4 weeks of age.

To get the pups eating on their own, mix some canned puppy or kitten food in a small amount of warm milk to make a slurry in a large low rimmed pan. A baking pan works well. Depending on the number and size of the puppies you may need more than one pan or you can platoon them. The slurry should cover only the bottom of the pan.

Take the puppies away from the momma for an hour or so to generate some hunger, prepare the food and milk mixture and then stand the pups in the pan. They will fall over and go thru some antics, lay down in the milk and so on, but in a very short time they will figure out what the deal is and start eating the mixture. You will need to lock up the momma when you feed the pups this way because if she can get to the pan she will eat the mixture and the pups get none. Momma is not being selfish; she just does not know that the food mixture is for the pups. After the pups finish then let momma in and she will finish the food and lick the pups clean. If the momma gets diarrhea from the lactose sugar in the milk you may want to use lactose free milk.

Stand the pups in the food mixture until they learn to eat over the side of the pan which may take a few days. Reduce the amount of milk, go to all canned food and you are on your way. The pups will still try to nurse but the momma usually will walk away. It is a good idea to have a place for the mama to retreat and the pups cannot get to her. The pups can be switched to dry food at 5 to 6 weeks.

Once the pups are eating solid food the momma will no longer clean up after them. To make your job of cleaning up easier put the pups on a thick mat of 30 or more sheets of newspaper. No blankets or towels because they are difficult to clean and there is going to be a lot of used food coming from those pups. The pups may crawl under the blankets and get lost or suffocate. The sheets of newspaper can be stripped off 2 or 3 at a time and just discarded.

The best time to put a puppy in a new home is on the day it turns 8 weeks, or if your state allows it, at 4 to 5 weeks. In most states the legal age to take a pup home is 8 weeks of age. If the pups are not in new homes at age 9 weeks they should each be put in an individual pen so that they only deal with humans and not other dogs. I have read about socializing with other dogs and fail to see the rationale. The puppy is going to be a pet living in the home with people. Therefore it should be socialized with humans and not other dogs. It can learn about other dogs later on.

If a pup is left with other dogs after 9 weeks it will often imprint on other dogs as their lifelong identification. In some cases they become so imprinted on other dogs that they fear humans and become "fear biters". Fear biters may accept and be okay around the family, but may well attack a visiting child or bite an adult who attempts to pet the animal. All of the dogs that I have dealt with for attacking an over—attentive child or an adult hand came into the family at an age of 4 months or later or were adopted as an adult with an unknown history.

A family dog should never growl or attempt to bite an over attentive child or a strange adult who is with the family. It should just move away. Attacking a stranger who has broken into your house is a different matter.

All of my dogs have been good watch dogs and they barked at strangers in the yard until they were told to stop. I made a point to have them meet the postman, delivery people and of course friends who visit the house. After the introduction the dogs welcomed the folks because they would always get a pat on the head.

OLD SPOUSE'S TALE: YOU CANNOT TEACH AN OLD DOG NEW TRICKS

THE TRUTH IS:

This tale came about when a wife asked her husband to use a new vacuum cleaner to vacuum the carpets. Since he did not want to do house cleaning he said there was no way he could learn to use that new fangled contraption—You can't teach an old dog new tricks said he and an Old Spouse's Tale was created.

Not true in the least unless it's a lazy spouse. Dogs, and other pets, can be taught new tricks or commands as long as they are in good health. Many working dogs such as sniffer dogs, field trial bird dogs, guard dogs, etc are not qualified to officially work in their appointed fields until they are 4 or 5 years old. And the training goes on continuously and the dogs get better and better as time goes on. Practice really improves their expertise in the field.

Dogs that are deaf either due to genetics, disease or old age will quickly learn hand signals—even the old dogs.

Talking parrots will continue to learn new words and tricks until very old age.

NOT AN OLD SPOUSE'S TALE: HOW TO DECIDE WHEN IT IS TIME FOR A MERCIFUL END

Pets grow old just like all other creatures and then they die. Hopefully, when your pet is old and in poor health you will find it has passed away peacefully in its sleep without you having to make any decisions.

But sometimes we know the pet is suffering and is it time to provide a merciful end? It is a very tough decision. Putting a pet to sleep is the worst part of Veterinary Medicine. I nearly always cried along with the family.

If I knew that someone was considering putting a pet to sleep and I had a relationship with the owner and the pet I would ask them that when they made the decision to take the pet to another Veterinarian. For me it was like ending the life of a good and trusting friend.

When I had to euthanatize my fabulous English Setter, Janie, I asked a trusted friend to go by the house and take her to the Veterinarian of his choice and have her put to sleep and cremated. It was one of the worst days of my life.

The question is how to make the decision. You have heard of Dr. Death, Dr. Jack Kevorkian, a Michigan pathologist who advocated letting terminal patients end their own life. When he assisted in a suicide Dr. Kevorkian arranged the apparatus and the patient was the one who had to push the button to end their own life.

If you could discuss voluntary end of life because of pain and suffering with your pet, and the method of suicide was explained, would your pet push the button?

If you think that the pet would push the button then it is time to go to the next step. If the pet has been cared for by one Veterinarian for a period of time it will be a favor to that Doctor to take the pet elsewhere for euthanasia. I suggest that just one person take the pet on its last visit so that the whole family is not crying in the Veterinary clinic. Everyone should say their goodbyes and then have just one person take the pet. Or do as I did and have a trusted friend take the pet in and when everyone comes home the pet is gone.

It is a most difficult decision and I empathize with anyone who has to make the decision. Assuming it is an older pet, then you did everything right during the life of the pet. Cancer, failing organs, paralysis and other old age conditions are an act of God and there was nothing that you could have done to change the outcome. Just be thankful that the pet had a long and joyful life in your family.